a little taste of...

china

a little taste of...

china

Recipes by Deh-Ta Hsiung and
 Nina Simonds
Photography by Jason Lowe
Additional text by Kay Halsey

MURDOCH
B O O K S

contents

SPECIAL FEATURES

dim sum **14**   tea **26**   chop suey **52**   hotpot **74**
chinese new year **110**   peking duck **128**
wok **158**   soy sauce **170**   chillies **186**
rice **200**   *char siu* **226**   noodles **242**

a little taste...

What distinguishes Chinese food from other cuisines is not only how it tastes, or the ingredients that give a Chinese meal its distinctive flavour, but how that meal is prepared and served. In China, food and life are intimately entwined — almost every ingredient seems imbued with medicinal or spiritual properties, and every dish symbolic or auspicious. Even the language is littered with food metaphors. The most masterful chefs are not just skilful with the wok, but compose meals that are a balance of ingredients, tastes and textures.

Even at the most informal dinner you can expect to be served at least five dishes. At home there is certainly no ceremony about the service, all the platters of food served at the same time, diners helping themselves and each other to food with their chopsticks. The Chinese attach great importance to their family and friends, and the experience of eating together maintains these relationships. The time taken preparing a meal is seen as a true labour of love, good food the catalyst for laughter, discussion and harmony.

Family meals tend to follow a fairly set pattern. No Chinese meal is complete without a soup, often medicinal, which is left on the table and drunk throughout the dinner or served just before dessert. In fact, the soup, usually a broth, can be the sole beverage available, for the Chinese traditionally drink tea only with dim sum, while alcohol is often reserved for eating out. The rice is the peg that the rest of the meal hangs from, though in the North it may be replaced with another staple like noodles or breads. Freshly steamed, it is scooped into individual rice bowls and topped up as needed.

To accompany the soup and rice are three or four dishes that must complement each other in appearance, aroma, flavour and texture. This can be done by choosing a different main ingredient for each, some vegetables, seafood, meat and poultry. The chef then selects from a variety of cooking techniques, perhaps steaming some broccoli, stir-frying prawns, preparing a platter of cold meats and slow-braising a chicken. Not only does this make for a balanced selection, with diverse textures, but means that all dishes are ready to be served at once, the cold meats and chicken prepared in advance, the broccoli and prawns cooked at the end.

But Chinese cooking is not just about the brilliance of its execution. A master chef must have an innate understanding of the nuances of Chinese food, choosing a dish for its medicinal or symbolic values, cooking with 'warming' ingredients to counter the effects of a wintry day or applying the universal principles of 'Yin-Yang' to the dinner table, creating a culinary harmony of cooling (Yin), heating (Yang) and neutral (Yin-Yang) dishes, which can even be matched to an individual's constitution.

a little taste of...

The classic Chinese tea house, set below sloping roofs in a calm, temple-like pagoda, is a rare find in today's China. Once the tea house held an important place in Chinese life, a men-only affair where deals were finalized and meetings held among the dark wooden stools and tables. It was a place not only of business, but of culture, live music or opera sounding from a tiny stage at the front. Storytellers and poets would mingle with tea-drinkers and the walls were covered with beautiful calligraphy hangings. Few of these tea houses survived past the Cultural Revolution, leaving only the working-class tea houses of the temples and People's Parks, serving inexpensive tea without ceremony, and the yum cha venues of southern China, where the dim sum has always been as important as the tea. However, in recent years, there has been a resurgence of interest in the tea house. Tea connoisseurs are beginning to congregate once more, choosing carefully from a selection of green, black and oolong varieties, each one beautifully prepared in a special clay teapot and served with traditional melon seeds, candied fruit, nuts, oranges or baskets of dim sum.

...the tea house

jiaozi

FILLING
300 g (11 oz) Chinese cabbage,
　finely chopped
1 teaspoon salt
450 g (1 lb) minced pork
100 g (3 bunches) Chinese garlic chives,
　finely chopped
2½ tablespoons light soy sauce
1 tablespoon Shaoxing rice wine

2 tablespoons roasted sesame oil
1 tablespoon finely chopped ginger
1 tablespoon cornflour (cornstarch)

50 round wheat dumpling wrappers
red rice vinegar or a dipping sauce
　(page 250)

Makes 50

To make the filling, put the cabbage and salt in a bowl and toss lightly to combine. Leave for 30 minutes. Squeeze all the water from the cabbage and put the cabbage in a bowl. Add the pork, chives, soy sauce, rice wine, sesame oil, ginger and cornflour. Stir until combined and drain off any excess liquid.

Place a heaped teaspoon of the filling in the centre of each wrapper. Spread a little water along the edge of the wrapper and fold the wrapper over to make a half-moon shape. Use your thumb and index finger to form small pleats along the sealed edge. With the other hand, press the two opposite edges together to seal. Place the dumplings on a baking tray that has been lightly dusted with cornflour. Do not allow the dumplings to sit for too long or they will go soggy.

Bring a large saucepan of water to the boil. Add half the dumplings, stirring immediately to prevent them from sticking together, and return to the boil. For the traditional method of cooking dumplings, add 250 ml (1 cup) cold water and continue cooking over high heat until the water boils. Add another 750 ml (3 cups) cold water and cook until the water boils again. Alternatively, cook the dumplings in the boiling water for 8–9 minutes. Remove the saucepan from the heat and drain the dumplings. Repeat with the remaining dumplings.

The dumplings can also be fried. Heat 1 tablespoon oil in a frying pan, add a single layer of dumplings and cook for 2 minutes, shaking the pan to make sure they don't stick. Add 75 ml water (⅓ cup), cover and steam for 2 minutes, then uncover and cook until the water has evaporated. Repeat with the remaining dumplings. Serve with red rice vinegar or a dipping sauce.

FILLING
180 g (6 oz) prawns (shrimp)
80 g (½ cup) peeled water chestnuts
450 g (1 lb) minced pork
2 tablespoons light soy sauce
1½ tablespoons Shaoxing
   rice wine
2 teaspoons roasted sesame oil
¼ teaspoon freshly ground
   black pepper
2 tablespoons finely chopped ginger

1 spring onion (scallion), finely chopped
1 egg white, lightly beaten
2 tablespoons cornflour (cornstarch)

30 square or round egg dumpling
   wrappers
1 tablespoon shrimp roe (optional)
dipping sauce (page 250)

Makes 30

To make the filling, peel and devein the prawns. Place in a tea towel and squeeze out as much moisture as possible, then roughly chop.

Blanch the water chestnuts in a pan of boiling water for 1 minute, then refresh in cold water. Drain, pat dry and roughly chop them. Place the prawns, water chestnuts, minced pork and the remaining filling ingredients in a large bowl and stir until well combined.

Place 1 tablespoon of filling in the centre of a dumpling wrapper. Gather up the edges of the wrapper around the filling. Holding the dumpling between your thumb and index finger, lightly squeeze it to form a 'waist', while at the same time pushing up the filling from the bottom with the other hand to create a flat base. Smooth the surface of the filling with a knife dipped in water.

Place the dumplings well apart in four steamers lined with greaseproof paper punched with holes. Put a small dot of shrimp roe in the centre of the filling in each dumpling if using. Cover the steamers and steam over simmering water in a wok, reversing the steamers halfway through, for 15 minutes. Serve with a dipping sauce.

siu mai

dim sum... Little Cantonese dumplings and snacks, dim sum are made to be eaten with cups of tea and are part of the great Chinese tea-drinking culture. Every region of China enjoys snacks, but the innovative chefs of the South took their dim sum one step further, creating hundreds of different types. So popular have they become, that what was once a little delicacy to accompany tea in a tea house can now be eaten as a whole meal.

Today's tea houses tend to be more like spit-and-sawdust working men's clubs than calm temples in which to eat and sip tea. They're places where a pot

of black *pu'er* (good for hangovers) and one or two basic dim sum accompany intense reading of the racing form. Any restaurant wanting to offer a serious selection of dim sum needs an army of specialist chefs, the economics of this creating huge establishments nicknamed 'dim sum palaces'. Dim sum kitchens usually play to a full house, and throughout the week these multi-level dining rooms fill up amazingly quickly with office workers who consider a hot lunch an essential part of the working day. At the weekends, families send grandparents off early to reserve a table, queues forming before midday to sample the week's best selection of dim sum.

Part of the appeal of dim sum is that it is played out to certain rituals. A cheongsam-clad hostess ushers the diner to a table as a waiter hastily clears away the previous diners' dishes. A choice of tea is offered, usually *pu'er*, jasmine or chrysanthemum. The waiter's other role is to refill teapots but only when the lid of the teapot has been lifted to one side. Dim sum etiquette dictates that diners mustn't pour their own tea before attending to everyone else. When a diner tops up another's teacup, the polite way to say thank you is to tap the table with two fingers. While more upmarket restaurants may offer a pencil to tick off orders from an order sheet, in most places the meal is very much self-service. Servers push trolleys stacked high with bamboo baskets of freshly made translucent prawn *har gau* and pork-stuffed *siu mai*, little dishes of spareribs and chicken feet. When flagged down and a dish chosen, the server marks the table's card with a stamp, or *chop*. At the end of the meal, the bill is calculated by tallying up the number of *chops*.

char siu bau

1 teaspoon oil
250 g (9 oz) barbecue pork
  (char siu), diced
3 teaspoons Shaoxing rice wine
1 teaspoon roasted sesame oil
2 tablespoons oyster sauce
2 teaspoons light soy sauce
3 teaspoons sugar
1 quantity basic yeast dough
  (page 251)
chilli sauce or recipe page 250

Makes 12 large or 24 small

Heat the oil in a wok. Add the pork, rice wine, sesame oil, oyster sauce, soy sauce and sugar and cook for 1 minute. Leave to cool.

Divide the dough into 12 or 24 portions, depending on how large you want your buns to be, and cover with a tea towel. Working with one portion at a time, press the dough into circles with the edges thinner than the centre.

Place 1 teaspoon of filling on the dough for a small bun or 3 teaspoons for a large bun. Draw the sides in to enclose the filling. Pinch the top together and put each bun on a square of greaseproof paper. When you get more proficient at making these, you may be able to get more filling into the buns, which will make them less doughy. Make sure that you seal them properly. The buns can also be turned over, then cooked the other way up so they look like round balls.

Place the buns well apart in three steamers. Cover and steam over simmering water in a wok, reversing the steamers halfway through, for 15 minutes, or until the buns are well risen and a skewer inserted into the centre comes out hot. Serve with chilli sauce.

600 g (3 cups) glutinous rice
4 large lotus leaves

FILLING
2 tablespoons dried shrimp
4 dried Chinese mushrooms
2 tablespoons oil
360 g (13 oz) skinless chicken breast
 fillet, cut into 1 cm (¼ in) cubes
1 garlic clove, crushed
2 Chinese sausages (lap cheong),
 thinly sliced

2 spring onions (scallions), thinly sliced
1 tablespoon oyster sauce
3 teaspoons light soy sauce
3 teaspoons sugar
1 teaspoon roasted sesame oil
1 tablespoon cornflour (cornstarch)
chilli sauce or recipe page 250

Makes 8

Place the rice in a bowl, cover with water and leave to soak overnight. Drain, then place the rice in a bamboo steamer lined with a tea towel. Steam, covered, over simmering water in a wok for 30–40 minutes, or until the rice is cooked.

Soak the lotus leaves in boiling water for 1 hour, or until softened. Shake dry and cut the leaves in half to give eight equal pieces.

To make the filling, soak the shrimp in boiling water for 1 hour, then drain. Soak the mushrooms in boiling water for 30 minutes, drain and squeeze out any excess water. Remove and discard the stems and finely chop the caps.

Heat a wok over high heat, add half the oil and heat until very hot. Stir-fry the chicken for 2–3 minutes, or until browned. Add the shrimp, mushrooms, garlic, sausage and spring onions. Stir-fry for 1–2 minutes. Add the oyster and soy sauces, sugar and sesame oil and toss well. Combine the cornflour with 200 ml (¾ cup) water, add to the sauce and simmer until thickened.

With wet hands, divide the rice into 16 balls. Place the lotus leaves on a work surface, put a ball of rice in the centre of each leaf and flatten the ball slightly, making a slight indentation in the middle. Spoon one-eighth of the filling onto each rice ball, top with another slightly flattened rice ball and smooth into one ball. Wrap up by folding the leaves over to form an envelope.

Place the parcels in three steamers. Cover and steam over simmering water in a wok, reversing the steamers halfway through, for 30 minutes. To serve, open up each leaf and eat straight from the leaf while hot with chilli sauce.

steamed glutinous rice in lotus leaves

har gau

FILLING
500 g (1 lb 2 oz) prawns (shrimp)
45 g (½ oz) pork or bacon fat,
 rind removed, finely chopped
40 g (¼ cup) fresh or tinned bamboo
 shoots, rinsed, drained and
 finely chopped
1 spring onion (scallion), finely chopped
1 teaspoon sugar
3 teaspoons light soy sauce
½ teaspoon roasted sesame oil
1 egg white, lightly beaten

1 teaspoon salt
1 tablespoon cornflour (cornstarch)

WRAPPER DOUGH
170 g (1⅓ cups) wheat starch
3 teaspoons cornflour (cornstarch)
2 teaspoons oil

chilli sauce or dipping sauce (page 250)

Makes 24

To make the filling, peel and devein the prawns and cut half of them into 1 cm (¼ in) chunks. Chop the remaining prawns until finely minced. Combine all prawns in a large bowl. Add the pork, bamboo shoots, spring onion, sugar, soy sauce, sesame oil, egg white, salt and cornflour. Mix well and drain off any excess liquid.

To make the dough, put the wheat starch, cornflour and oil in a small bowl. Add 250 ml (1 cup) boiling water and mix. Add a little extra wheat starch if the dough is too sticky.

Roll the dough into a long cylinder, divide it into 24 pieces and cover with a hot damp tea towel. Working with one portion at a time, roll out the dough using a rolling pin. Roll the dough into a 9–10 cm (3½–4 in) round between two pieces of oiled plastic wrap. Fill each wrapper as you make it.

Place a heaped teaspoon of the filling in the centre of each wrapper. Spread a little water along the edge of the wrapper and fold the wrapper over to make a half-moon shape. Use your thumb and index finger to form small pleats along the top edge. With the other hand, press the two opposite edges together to seal. Place the har gau in four steamers lined with greaseproof paper punched with holes. Cover the har gau as you make them to prevent them from drying out.

Cover and steam the har gau over simmering water in a wok, reversing the steamers halfway through, for 6–8 minutes, or until the wrappers are translucent. Serve with soy sauce, chilli sauce or a dipping sauce.

FILLING

5 tablespoons light soy sauce
2 teaspoons roasted sesame oil
3½ tablespoons Shaoxing rice wine
1½ teaspoons cornflour (cornstarch)
450 g (1 lb) centre-cut pork loin, trimmed
 and cut into very thin strips
6 dried Chinese mushrooms
½ teaspoon freshly ground black pepper
4 tablespoons oil
1 tablespoon finely chopped ginger
3 garlic cloves, finely chopped
130 g (5 oz) Chinese cabbage,
 finely shredded

150 g (1 cup) carrot, finely shredded
30 g (1 bunch) Chinese garlic chives,
 cut into 2 cm (¾ in) lengths
180 g (2 cups) bean sprouts

1 egg yolk
2 tablespoons plain (all-purpose) flour
20 square spring-roll wrappers
oil, for deep-frying
plum sauce

Makes 20

To make the filling, combine 2 tablespoons of the soy sauce and half the sesame oil with 1½ tablespoons of the rice wine and 1 teaspoon of the cornflour. Add the pork and toss to coat. Marinate in the fridge for 20 minutes. Meanwhile, soak the mushrooms in boiling water for 30 minutes, then drain and squeeze out any excess water. Remove and discard the stems and shred the caps. Combine the remaining soy sauce, sesame oil and cornflour with the pepper.

Heat a wok over high heat, add half the oil and heat until very hot. Add the pork mixture and stir-fry for 2 minutes, or until cooked. Remove and drain. Reheat the wok over high heat, add the remaining oil and heat until very hot. Stir-fry the mushrooms, ginger and garlic for 15 seconds. Add the cabbage and carrot and toss. Pour in the remaining rice wine, then stir-fry for 1 minute. Add the chives and sprouts and stir-fry for 1 minute. Add the pork mixture and soy sauce mixture and cook until thickened. Drain in a colander for 5 minutes.

Combine the egg yolk, flour and 3 tablespoons water. Place 2 tablespoons of filling on the corner of a wrapper. Spread some of the yolk mixture on the opposite corner. Fold over one corner and start rolling. Fold in the other corners, roll up and press to secure. Repeat with the remaining wrappers.

Fill a wok to one-quarter full with oil. Heat the oil to 190°C (375°F/Gas 5). Cook the spring rolls in two batches, turning constantly, for 5 minutes, or until golden. Remove and drain on paper towels. Serve with plum sauce.

spring rolls

tea... One of China's icons, tea is very much part of its culture, customs and legend. The tea plant is native only to Southwest China and Assam in India, and it was from the mountains of China that tea travelled to, and wooed, the great tea-drinking nations of Japan, Europe and India.

It is hard to know when tea was discovered as, unlike in India, the Chinese appear to have used wild tea leaves as a tonic for thousands of years. But, by the time the 'Father of Tea', Lu Yu, wrote his book, *Tea Classic*, in 780, growing, blending and brewing rituals, along with elaborate ceremonies that made it the favoured drink of the rich, had elevated tea to the status of a cult. A meeting place

was even invented to indulge this passion — the tea house — which helped fuel the poetry, ceremony and snobbery that surrounded the tea-drinking elite.

As the Chinese learnt to cultivate tea and it became plentiful, the poorer classes became addicted, too. The rituals and ceremony do survive, and tea preparation is extremely important to the Chinese connoisseur, but tea is also now the fuel of the working classes. Shops, trains, hotels and waiting rooms provide a thermos flask of hot water to keep tea-cups, or even just a screw-top jar, constantly topped up.

Tea, despite its countless variations, is gathered from just one plant, *Camellia sinensis*. Differences in taste can be a result, like wine, of growing the plant in

variable altitudes, soils and climates, but the most important factors by far are the way the plant is picked and processed. The purest forms are green and, more rarely, white teas, where the leaves are dried before they have a chance to ferment and oxidize. Highly prized oolong teas from Fujian and Taiwan are semi-fermented, with the scent of green and the flavour of black, while black teas are fully fermented and were the only teas capable of making the long sea journey to Europe. The Chinese also love tisanes, flower teas, which can be heart-stoppingly beautiful.

turnip cake

900 g (2 lb) Chinese turnip, grated
30 g (1 oz) dried shrimp
20 g (2 cups) dried Chinese mushrooms
150 g (6 oz) Chinese sausage
    (lap cheong)
1 tablespoon oil
3 spring onions (scallions), thinly sliced
3 teaspoons sugar
3 teaspoons Shaoxing rice wine

¼ teaspoon freshly ground
    white pepper
2 tablespoons finely chopped coriander
    (cilantro)
280 g (1⅔ cups) rice flour
oil, for frying

Makes 6

Place the turnip in a large bowl and cover with boiling water for 5 minutes. Drain, reserving any liquid, then leave the turnip to drain in a colander. When it is cool enough to handle, squeeze out any excess liquid. Place in a bowl.

Soak the dried shrimp in boiling water for 1 hour, then drain, adding any soaking liquid to the reserved turnip liquid.

Soak the mushrooms in boiling water for 30 minutes, then drain, adding any soaking liquid to the reserved turnip liquid. Squeeze out any excess water from the mushrooms. Remove and discard the stems and finely dice the caps.

Place the sausage on a plate in a steamer. Cover and steam over simmering water in a wok for 10 minutes, then finely dice it.

Heat a wok over high heat, add the oil and heat until very hot. Stir-fry the sausage for 1 minute, then add the shrimp and mushrooms and stir-fry for 2 minutes, or until fragrant. Add the spring onions, sugar, rice wine and pepper, then add the turnip, coriander and rice flour and toss to combine. Pour in 500 ml (2 cups) of the reserved liquid and mix well.

Place the mixture in a greased and lined 25 cm (10 in) square cake tin (or in two smaller tins if your steamers are small). Place the tin in a steamer. Cover and steam over simmering water in a wok for 1¼–1½ hours, or until firm, replenishing with boiling water during cooking. Remove the tin and cool in the fridge overnight. Take the cake from the tin and cut into 5 cm (2 in) squares that are 1 cm (¼ in) thick.

Heat a wok over high heat, add 2 tablespoons of the oil and heat until very hot. Cook the turnip cakes in batches until golden and crispy.

1 kg (2 lb 4 oz) Chinese-style
   pork spareribs
1 egg, beaten
2–3 tablespoons plain
   (all-purpose) flour
oil, for deep-frying
2 spring onions (scallions),
   finely chopped
2 small red chillies, finely chopped

MARINADE
½ teaspoon ground Sichuan peppercorns
½ teaspoon five-spice powder
½ teaspoon salt
1 tablespoon light soy sauce
1 tablespoon Shaoxing rice wine
¼ teaspoon roasted sesame oil

Serves 4

Ask the butcher to cut the slab of spareribs crosswise into thirds that measure 4–5 cm (1½–2 in) in length, or use a cleaver to do so yourself. Cut the ribs between the bones to separate them.

To make the marinade, combine the ingredients in a bowl. Add the ribs and toss lightly. Marinate in the fridge for at least 3 hours, or overnight.

Mix the egg, flour and a little water to form a smooth batter the consistency of thickened cream. Fill a wok one-quarter full of oil. Heat the oil to 180°C (350°F/Gas 4), or until a piece of bread fries golden brown in 15 seconds when dropped in the oil. Dip the ribs in the batter and fry in batches for 5 minutes until they are crisp and golden, stirring to separate them, then remove and drain. Reheat the oil and fry the ribs for 1 minute to darken the colour. Remove and drain on paper towels.

Soak the spring onions and chillies in the hot oil (with the heat off) for 2 minutes. Remove with a wire strainer or slotted spoon and sprinkle over the ribs.

spicy spareribs

tofu rolls

4 dried Chinese mushrooms
100 g (⅓ cup) fresh or tinned bamboo
   shoots, rinsed and drained
1 small carrot
3 tablespoons oil
300 g (11 oz) firm tofu, drained
   and diced
200 g (2¼ cups) bean sprouts
½ teaspoon salt
½ teaspoon sugar

2 spring onions (scallions), finely shredded
1 tablespoon light soy sauce
1 teaspoon roasted sesame oil
1 tablespoon plain (all-purpose) flour
12 sheets soft or dried tofu skins
oil, for deep-frying
red rice vinegar, soy sauce or dipping
   sauce (page 250)

Makes 12

Soak the dried mushrooms in boiling water for 30 minutes, then drain and squeeze out any excess water. Remove and discard the stems and finely shred the caps. Cut the bamboo shoots and carrot into thin strips about the size of the bean sprouts.

Heat a wok over high heat, add the oil and heat until very hot. Stir-fry the carrot, tofu and bean sprouts for 1 minute. Add the mushrooms and bamboo shoots, toss, then add the salt, sugar and spring onions. Stir-fry for 1 minute, then add the soy sauce and sesame oil, and blend well. Remove the mixture from the wok and drain off the excess liquid. Leave to cool. Combine the flour with a little cold water to make a paste.

If you are using dried tofu skins, soak them in cold water until they are soft. Peel off a sheet of tofu skin and trim to a 15 x 18 cm (6 x 8 in) rectangle. Place 2 tablespoons of the filling at one end of the skin, and roll up to make a neat parcel, folding the sides in as you roll. Brush the skin with some of the flour paste to seal the flap. Repeat with the remaining tofu skins and filling.

Fill a wok to one-quarter full of oil. Heat the oil to 180°C (350°F/Gas 4), or until a piece of bread fries golden brown in 15 seconds when dropped in the oil. Cook the rolls in batches for 3–4 minutes, or until golden. Serve with some red rice vinegar, soy sauce or a dipping sauce.

a little taste of...

Chinese home-style cooking is generally based around rice and two, even three, filling bowls can be devoured as lunch or dinner. The collection of small dishes that accompany this rice are seen almost as a garnish, sometimes no more than a little pickle or dried shrimp. Most Chinese food is a combination of fresh ingredients and a few basic flavourings. Most of the recipes can be prepared quickly from the kitchen's store cupboard, filling the house with the wonderful smells of soy sauce, ginger, spring onions, garlic and toasted sesame oil. The Chinese buy fresh ingredients daily, favouring inexpensive tofu, eggs, vegetables and squid for cooking at home. Medicinal herbs and soothing ginger are bought to be infused in soups, especially in the winter, and seasonal fresh fruit sliced for dessert. Skilful home cooks will also prepare their own 'master stock', kept topped up with scraps and bones, which adds a unique, rich taste to their food. Pickles are made whenever there is a glut of vegetables, and handmade sausages are hung in the kitchen to dry.

...home-style cooking

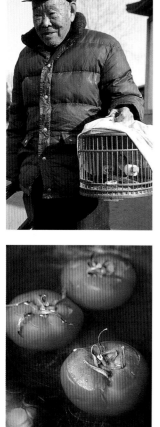

tomato and egg soup

250 g (9 oz) firm ripe tomatoes
2 eggs
1 spring onion (scallion), finely chopped
1 tablespoon oil
1 litre (4 cups) vegetable or chicken and
   meat stock or recipes page 249
1 tablespoon light soy sauce
1 tablespoon cornflour (cornstarch)

Serves 4

Score a cross in the bottom of each tomato. Plunge into boiling water for 20 seconds, then drain and peel the skin away from the cross. Cut into slices or thin wedges, trimming off the core. Beat the eggs with a pinch of salt and a few pieces of spring onion.

Heat a wok over high heat, add the oil and heat until very hot. Stir-fry the spring onion for a few seconds to flavour the oil, then pour in the stock and bring to the boil. Add the tomato and return to the boil. Add the soy sauce and slowly pour in the beaten eggs, stirring as you pour. Return to the boil.

Combine the cornflour with enough water to make a paste, add to the soup and simmer until thickened.

250 g (9 oz) skinless chicken breast
   fillet, minced
150 ml (¾ cup) Shaoxing rice wine
400 g (14 oz) tinned creamed corn
1.5 litres (6 cups) chicken stock
   or recipe page 249
1 teaspoon salt
2½ tablespoons cornflour (cornstarch)
2 egg whites, lightly beaten
1 teaspoon roasted sesame oil

Serves 6

Place the chicken in a bowl, add 3 tablespoons of the rice wine and stir to combine. In a large clay pot or saucepan, combine the creamed corn, stock, remaining rice wine and salt. Bring to the boil, stirring. Add the chicken and stir to separate the meat. Return to the boil and skim any scum from the surface.

Combine the cornflour with enough water to make a paste, add to the soup and simmer until thickened. Remove from the heat. Mix 2 tablespoons water into the egg white, then slowly add to the clay pot in a thin stream around the edge of the pan. Stir once or twice, then add the sesame oil. Check the seasoning, adding more salt if necessary. Serve immediately.

cantonese corn soup

ten-treasure soup

400 g (14 oz) Chinese cabbage
2 tablespoons oil
4 garlic cloves, smashed with
 the flat side of a cleaver
130 ml (½ cup) Shaoxing rice wine
1.5 litres (6 cups) chicken stock
 or recipe page 249
1 teaspoon salt
250 g (9 oz) centre-cut pork loin, trimmed
2 teaspoons light soy sauce
½ teaspoon roasted sesame oil
450 g (1 lb) prawns (shrimp)

3 slices ginger, smashed with
 the flat side of a cleaver
30 g (1 oz) bean thread noodles
6 dried Chinese mushrooms
450 g (1 lb) firm tofu, drained and cut
 into 2.5 cm (1 in) squares
2 carrots, cut into 2 cm (¾ in) pieces
200 g (½ bunch) baby spinach leaves
3 spring onions (scallions), green part only,
 cut diagonally into 1 cm (¼ in) lengths

Serves 6

Remove the stems from the cabbage and cut the leaves into 5 cm (2 in) squares. Separate the hard cabbage pieces from the leafy ones. Heat a wok over high heat, add the oil and heat until very hot. Add the hard cabbage and the garlic. Toss over high heat, adding 1 tablespoon of the rice wine. Stir-fry for several minutes, then add the leafy cabbage. Stir-fry for 1 minute, add 4 tablespoons of the rice wine, the stock and half of the salt. Bring to the boil, then reduce the heat to low and cook for 30 minutes. Transfer to a clay pot or saucepan.

Cut the pork across the grain into slices about 2 mm (⅛ in) thick. Place the pork in a bowl, add the soy sauce and sesame oil, and toss lightly. Marinate in the fridge for 20 minutes.

Peel and devein the prawns, then place in a bowl with the ginger, remaining rice wine and salt and toss lightly. Marinate in the fridge for 20 minutes. Remove and discard the ginger.

Soak the noodles in hot water for 10 minutes, then drain and cut into 15 cm (6 in) lengths. Soak the dried mushrooms in boiling water for 30 minutes, then drain and squeeze out any excess water. Remove and discard the stems.

Arrange the pork slices, tofu, mushrooms, noodles and carrot in separate piles on top of the cabbage in the casserole, leaving some space in the centre for the prawns and spinach. Cover and cook over medium heat for 20 minutes. Arrange the prawns and spinach in the centre and sprinkle with the spring onions. Cover and cook for 5 minutes, or until the prawns are pink and cooked through. Season with salt if necessary. Serve directly from the pot.

4 dried Chinese mushrooms
2 tablespoons dried black fungus
   (wood ears)
100 g (4 oz) lean pork, thinly shredded
1 tablespoon cornflour (cornstarch)
120 g (5 oz) firm tofu, drained
50 g (¼ cup) fresh or tinned bamboo
   shoots, rinsed and drained
1 litre (4 cups) chicken and meat stock
   or recipe page 249
1 tablespoon Shaoxing rice wine
2 tablespoons light soy sauce
1–2 tablespoons Chinese black rice vinegar
2 eggs, beaten
1–2 teaspoons freshly ground
   white pepper
1 chopped spring onion (scallion)

Serves 4

Soak the dried mushrooms in boiling water for 30 minutes, then drain and squeeze out any excess water. Remove and discard the stems and shred the caps. Soak the dried black fungus in cold water for 20 minutes, then drain and squeeze out any excess water. Shred the black fungus.

Combine the pork, a pinch of salt and 1 teaspoon of the cornflour. Thinly shred the tofu and bamboo shoots to the same size as the pork.

Bring the stock to the boil in a large clay pot or saucepan. Add the pork and stir to separate the meat, then add the mushroom, black fungus, tofu and bamboo. Return to the boil and add the salt, rice wine, soy sauce and vinegar. Slowly pour in the egg, whisking to form thin threads, and cook for 1 minute. Combine the remaining cornflour with enough water to make a paste, add to the soup and simmer until thickened. Put the pepper in a bowl, pour in the soup and stir. Garnish with the spring onion.

hot-and-sour soup

whole fish with yellow bean sauce

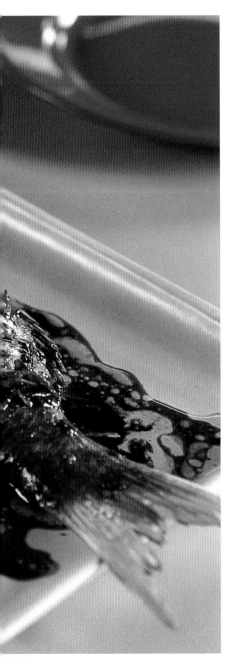

750 g–1 kg (1 lb 10 oz–2 lb 4 oz) fish,
  such as carp, bream, grouper or
  sea bass
1 tablespoon light soy sauce
1 tablespoon Shaoxing rice wine
oil, for deep-frying
1 tablespoon shredded ginger
2 spring onions (scallions), thinly shredded

1 teaspoon sugar
1 tablespoon dark soy sauce
2 tablespoons yellow bean sauce
100 ml (½ cup) chicken and meat stock
  or recipe page 249
½ teaspoon roasted sesame oil

Serves 4

If you do manage to buy a swimming (live) fish, then ask the fishmonger to gut it through the gills. This is harder than gutting through the stomach, but leaves the fish looking whole. If you are gutting the fish yourself, make a cut from the throat to the tail and pull out the guts through the stomach. Remove any scales with a fish scaler or the back of a knife. Check that the gills have been cut out, then rinse the fish under cold, running water and drain thoroughly in a colander.

Diagonally score both sides of the fish, cutting through as far as the bone at intervals of 2 cm (¾ in). Place the fish in a shallow dish with the light soy sauce and rice wine and leave to marinate for 10–15 minutes, then drain off any liquid, reserving the marinade.

Fill a wok to one-quarter full of oil. Heat the oil to 190°C (375°F/Gas 5), or until a piece of bread fries golden brown in 10 seconds when dropped in the oil. Holding the fish by its tail, gently and carefully lower it into the oil, bending the body so the cuts open up. Cook for 5 minutes, or until golden brown, tilting the wok so the entire fish is cooked in the oil. Remove and drain on crumpled paper towels and keep warm in a low oven. Pour the oil from the wok, leaving 1½ tablespoons.

Reheat the reserved oil over high heat until very hot. Add the ginger, spring onions, sugar, dark soy sauce, yellow bean sauce and reserved marinade. Stir for a few seconds, add the stock, bring to the boil and add the fish. Cook for 4–5 minutes, basting constantly and turning the fish once after 2 minutes.

Turn the fish over and sprinkle with the sesame oil. Serve with the sauce poured over.

2 tablespoons light soy sauce
1 tablespoon dark soy sauce
3 tablespoons Shaoxing rice wine
2 tablespoons rock (lump) sugar
2 teaspoons five-spice powder
1 spring onion (scallion), finely chopped
2 teaspoons finely chopped ginger
450 g (1 lb) firm white fish fillets, such as
   haddock, monkfish or sea bass, skin on
300 ml (1¼ cups) chicken and meat stock
   or recipe page 249
oil, for deep-frying
coriander (cilantro) leaves

Serves 6

Mix together the soy sauces, rice wine, sugar, five-spice powder, spring onion and ginger. Pat dry the fish and leave in the marinade for 1 hour. Transfer the fish and marinade to a clay pot or saucepan. Add the stock and bring to the boil. Reduce the heat and simmer gently for 10 minutes, or until the fish is cooked through, then drain the fish, reserving the marinade.

Fill a wok to one-quarter full of oil. Heat the oil to 190°C (375°F/Gas 5), or until a piece of bread fries golden brown in 10 seconds when dropped in the oil. Carefully cook the fish in batches for 3–4 minutes, or until golden and crisp (it will spit a little). Remove the fish from the oil and return it to the marinade. Leave to cool for 2–3 hours.

Remove the fish from the marinade and leave to dry for a few minutes. Cut the fish into thin slices and serve cold, sprinkled with coriander leaves.

The marinade can be reused as a master sauce (see page 253).

smoked fish

ma po tofu

750 g (1 lb 10 oz) soft or firm tofu, drained
250 g (9 oz) minced beef or pork
2 tablespoons dark soy sauce
1½ tablespoons Shaoxing rice wine
½ teaspoon roasted sesame oil
2 teaspoons Sichuan peppercorns
1 tablespoon oil
2 spring onions (scallions), finely chopped
2 garlic cloves, finely chopped

2 teaspoons finely chopped ginger
1 tablespoon chilli bean paste (toban jiang), or to taste
250 ml (1 cup) chicken and meat stock or recipe page 249
1½ teaspoons cornflour (cornstarch)
1 spring onion (scallion), finely shredded

Serves 6

Cut the tofu into cubes. Place the meat in a bowl with 2 teaspoons of the soy sauce, 2 teaspoons of the rice wine and the sesame oil, and toss lightly. Dry-fry the peppercorns in a wok or pan until brown and aromatic, then crush lightly.

Heat a wok over high heat, add the oil and heat until very hot. Stir-fry the meat until browned, mashing and chopping to separate the pieces. Remove the meat with a wire sieve or slotted spoon and heat the oil until any liquid from the meat has evaporated. Add the spring onion, garlic and ginger and stir-fry for 10 seconds, or until fragrant. Add the chilli bean paste and stir-fry for 5 seconds.

Combine the stock with the remaining soy sauce and rice wine. Add to the wok, bring to the boil, then add the tofu and meat. Return to the boil, reduce the heat to medium and cook for 5 minutes, or until the sauce has reduced by a quarter. If you are using soft tofu, do not stir or it will break up.

Combine the cornflour with enough water to make a paste, add to the sauce and simmer until thickened. Season if necessary. Serve sprinkled with the spring onion and Sichuan peppercorns.

chop suey... Chinese cuisine is the world's take-away food. One well-known favourite dish, chop suey, which is found in almost every country, is now imported back to China as 'American chop suey'. And while most of this take-away food has its origins in China, dishes have been so adapted to local tastes that they somehow manage to be exotic while also strangely familiar.

Chinese food is one of the world's great cuisines, and as such, has huge appeal. But it was Chinese immigration, especially in the 19th century, that made it popular overseas. The first restaurants were a response to the demand by immigrants for the food of their homeland. Most immigrants were Cantonese and few were professional chefs, so the result was peasant dishes made from whatever ingredients were available. When Westerners began sampling this food, Chinese restaurants seized an opportunity, adapting dishes in line with what these new customers seemed to favour: prawn toasts, sweet-and-sour pork balls with chunks of pineapple, fried rice, crispy chow mein and chop suey. With a liberal dousing of soy sauce, this cuisine quickly became distinct from its Cantonese origins.

Indeed, many Western restaurants began to lead a double life. The English menu bore no resemblance to the Chinese — the kitchen would send out totally different food to each of their two clienteles. For many years, non-Chinese customers barely tasted authentic Chinese cooking at all. Only recently have things begun to change. The sharp rise in non-Cantonese immigration finally introduced Western diners to the flavours of other regions, with dishes braised in soy, rice wine, vinegar and chilli. And in Cantonese restaurants, increasingly cosmopolitan Western customers demanded to order from the Chinese menu. As a result, restaurants are cooking for a new clientele that wants to eat the real food of China as well as, just sometimes, the chop suey they grew up with.

350 g (12 oz) skinless chicken breast fillet
3 tablespoons light soy sauce
3 tablespoons Shaoxing rice wine
2 teaspoons roasted sesame oil
1 tablespoon cornflour (cornstarch)
120 g (¾ cup) peeled water chestnuts
3 tablespoons oil
450 g (1 bunch) baby spinach leaves
½ teaspoon salt
3 garlic cloves, finely chopped

120 g unsalted peanuts
1 spring onion (scallion), finely chopped
1 tablespoon finely chopped ginger
1 teaspoon chilli sauce or recipe page 250
1 tablespoon sugar
1 teaspoon Chinese black rice vinegar
60 ml (¼ cup) chicken stock or recipe
 page 249

Serves 6

Cut the chicken into 2.5 cm (1 in) cubes. Place the cubes in a bowl, add
2 tablespoons of the soy sauce, 2 tablespoons of the rice wine, 1 teaspoon
of the sesame oil and 2 teaspoons of the cornflour, and toss lightly. Marinate
in the fridge for at least 20 minutes.

Blanch the water chestnuts in a pan of boiling water, then refresh in cold
water. Drain, pat dry and cut into thin slices.

Heat a wok over high heat, add 1 teaspoon of the oil and heat until very
hot. Stir-fry the spinach, salt, 2 teaspoons of the garlic and 2 teaspoons of
the rice wine, turning constantly, until the spinach is just becoming limp.
Remove the spinach from the wok, arrange around the edge of a platter,
cover and keep warm.

Reheat the wok over high heat, add 1 tablespoon of the oil and heat until
very hot. Stir-fry half the chicken pieces, turning constantly, until the meat is
cooked. Remove with a wire sieve or slotted spoon and drain. Repeat with
1 tablespoon of oil and the remaining chicken. Wipe out the pan.

Dry-fry the peanuts in the wok or a saucepan until browned.

Reheat the wok over high heat, add the remaining oil and heat until very hot.
Stir-fry the spring onion, ginger, remaining garlic and chilli sauce for 10 seconds,
or until fragrant. Add the sliced water chestnuts and stir-fry for 15 seconds, or
until heated through. Combine the sugar, black vinegar, chicken stock and
remaining soy sauce, rice wine, sesame oil and cornflour, add to the sauce
and simmer until thickened. Add the cooked chicken and the peanuts. Toss
lightly to coat with the sauce. Transfer to the centre of the platter and serve.

kung pao chicken

white cut chicken

1.25 kg (2 lb 12 oz) chicken
2 spring onions (scallions), each tied
    in a knot
3 slices ginger, smashed with the
    flat side of a cleaver
3 tablespoons Shaoxing rice wine
1 tablespoon salt

DIPPING SAUCE
4 tablespoons dark soy sauce
1 tablespoon sugar
1 spring onion (scallion), finely chopped
1 garlic clove, finely chopped
1 teaspoon finely chopped ginger
1 teaspoon roasted sesame oil

Serves 4

Rinse the chicken, drain, and remove any fat from the cavity opening and
around the neck. Cut off and discard the parson's nose. Bring 1.5 litres (6 cups)
water to a rolling boil in a clay pot or casserole, and gently lower the chicken
into the water with the breast side up. Add the spring onion, ginger and rice
wine, return to the boil, then add the salt and simmer, covered, for 15 minutes.

Turn off the heat and leave the chicken to cool in the liquid for 5–6 hours,
without lifting the lid.

About 30 minutes before serving time, remove and drain the chicken. Using
a cleaver, cut the chicken through the bones into bite-size pieces.

To make the dipping sauce, combine the soy sauce, sugar, spring onion,
garlic, ginger and sesame oil with a little of the cooking liquid. Divide the
sauce among small saucers, one for each person. Each chicken piece is
dipped before eating. (Alternatively, pour the sauce over the chicken before
serving, but use light soy sauce instead of dark soy sauce so as not to spoil
the 'whiteness' of the chicken.)

1½ cucumbers
1 teaspoon salt
30 g (1 oz) bean thread noodles
1 teaspoon roasted sesame oil
250 g (9 oz) cooked chicken, cut into shreds
2 spring onions (scallions), green part
   only, finely sliced, to serve

PEANUT DRESSING
60 g (¼ cup) smooth peanut butter
1 teaspoon light soy sauce
1½ tablespoons sugar
2 teaspoons Chinese black rice vinegar
1 tablespoon Shaoxing rice wine
1 tablespoon roasted sesame oil
1 spring onion (scallion), finely chopped
1 tablespoon finely chopped ginger
1 teaspoon chilli sauce or recipe page 250
2½ tablespoons chicken stock or
   recipe page 249

OR

SESAME DRESSING
¼ teaspoon Sichuan peppercorns
3 garlic cloves
2 cm (¾ in) piece ginger
½ teaspoon chilli sauce or recipe page 250
3 tablespoons toasted sesame paste
2 tablespoons roasted sesame oil
2½ tablespoons light soy sauce
1 tablespoon Shaoxing rice wine
1 tablespoon Chinese black rice vinegar
1 tablespoon sugar
3 tablespoons chicken stock
   or recipe page 249

Serves 6

Slice the cucumbers lengthways and remove the seeds. Cut each half crossways into thirds, then cut each piece lengthways into thin slices about 5 cm (2 in) long. Place the slices in a bowl, add the salt, toss, and set aside for 20 minutes.

To make the peanut dressing, combine the peanut butter, soy sauce, sugar, vinegar, rice wine, sesame oil, spring onion, ginger, chilli sauce and stock in a blender. Blend to a smooth paste, adding water if needed. Pour into a bowl.

To make the sesame dressing, put the peppercorns in a frying pan and cook over medium heat, stirring occasionally, for 7–8 minutes. Cool slightly, then crush into a powder. Combine the garlic, ginger, chilli sauce, sesame paste, sesame oil, soy sauce, rice wine, vinegar, sugar and stock in a blender and blend to a smooth paste. Stir in the peppercorn powder. Pour into a bowl.

Soak the noodles in hot water for 10 minutes, drain and cut into 8 cm (3 in) lengths. Blanch in a pan of boiling water for 3 minutes, refresh in cold water and drain. Toss noodles in sesame oil and put on a plate. Put the cucumber on top, then add chicken shreds. Pour over dressing and sprinkle with the spring onion.

bang bang chicken

lemon chicken

500 g (1 lb 2oz) skinless chicken
   breast fillet
1 tablespoon light soy sauce
1 tablespoon Shaoxing rice wine
1 spring onion (scallion), finely chopped
1 tablespoon finely chopped ginger
1 garlic clove, finely chopped
1 egg, lightly beaten
100 g (¾ cup) cornflour (cornstarch)
oil, for deep-frying

LEMON SAUCE
2 tablespoons lemon juice
2 teaspoons sugar
½ teaspoon salt
½ teaspoon roasted sesame oil
3 tablespoons chicken stock or recipe
   page 249 or water
½ teaspoon cornflour (cornstarch)

Serves 6

Cut the chicken into slices. Place in a bowl, add the soy sauce, rice wine, spring onion, ginger and garlic, and toss lightly. Marinate in the fridge for at least 1 hour, or overnight.

Add the egg to the chicken mixture and toss lightly to coat. Drain any excess egg and coat the chicken pieces with the cornflour. The easiest way to do this is to put the chicken and cornflour in a plastic bag and shake it.

Fill a wok to one-quarter full of oil. Heat the oil to 190°C (375°F/Gas 5), or until a piece of bread fries golden brown in 10 seconds when dropped in the oil. Add half the chicken, a piece at a time, and fry, stirring constantly, for 3½–4 minutes, or until golden brown. Remove with a wire sieve or slotted spoon and drain. Repeat with the remaining chicken. Reheat the oil and return all the chicken to the wok. Cook until crisp and golden brown. Drain the chicken. Pour off the oil and wipe out the wok.

To make the lemon sauce, combine the lemon juice, sugar, salt, sesame oil, stock and cornflour.

Reheat the wok over medium heat until hot, add the lemon sauce and stir constantly until thickened. Add the chicken and toss lightly in the sauce.

450 g (1 lb) minced pork
1 egg white
4 spring onions (scallions), finely chopped
1 tablespoon Shaoxing rice wine
1 teaspoon grated ginger
1 tablespoon light soy sauce
2 teaspoons sugar
1 teaspoon roasted sesame oil
300 g (½ bunch) bok choy (pak choi)
1 tablespoon cornflour (cornstarch)
oil, for frying
500 ml (2 cups) chicken and meat stock
   or recipe page 249

Serves 4

Put the pork and egg white in a food processor and process briefly until you have a fluffy mixture, or mash the pork in a large bowl and gradually stir in the egg white, beating the mixture well until it is fluffy. Add the spring onions, rice wine, ginger, soy sauce, sugar and sesame oil, season with salt and white pepper, and process or beat again briefly. Fry a small portion of the mixture and taste it, seasoning again if necessary. Divide the mixture into walnut-size balls.

Separate the bok choy leaves and place in the bottom of a clay pot or casserole dish.

Dust the meatballs with the cornflour. Heat a wok over high heat, add 1 cm (¼ in) oil and heat until very hot. Cook the meatballs in batches until they are browned all over. Drain well and add to the clay pot in an even layer. Pour off the oil and wipe out the wok.

Reheat the wok over high heat until very hot, add the chicken stock and heat until it is boiling. Pour over the meatballs. Cover and bring very slowly to the boil. Simmer gently with the lid slightly open for 1½ hours, or until the meatballs are very tender. Serve the meatballs in the dish they were cooked in.

lion's head
meatballs

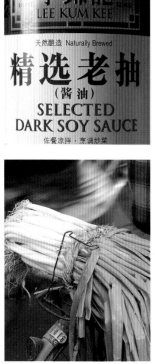

red-cooked pork

1.5 kg (3 lb 5 oz) pork leg, with bone in
and rind on
4 spring onions (scallions), each tied
in a knot
4 slices ginger, smashed with the flat
side of a cleaver
200 ml (¾ cup) dark soy sauce
4 tablespoons Shaoxing rice wine
1 teaspoon five-spice powder
50 g (2 oz) rock (lump) sugar

Serves 8

Scrape the pork rind to make sure it is free of any bristles. Blanch the pork in a pan of boiling water for 4–5 minutes. Rinse the pork and place in a clay pot or casserole dish with 600 ml (2½ cups) water, the spring onions, ginger, soy sauce, rice wine, five-spice powder and sugar. Bring to the boil, then reduce the heat and simmer, covered, for 2½–3 hours, turning several times, until the meat is very tender and falling from the bone.

If there is too much liquid, remove the pork and reduce the sauce by boiling it for 10–15 minutes. Slice the pork and serve with the sauce poured over it.

600 g (1 lb 5 oz) centre-cut pork loin,
  trimmed
1 egg
100 g (¾ cup) cornflour (cornstarch)
1 tablespoon oil
1 onion, cubed
1 red capsicum (pepper), cubed or cut into
  small triangles
2 spring onions (scallions), cut into
  2 cm (¾ in) lengths
150 g (⅔ cup) Chinese pickles
250 ml (1 cup) clear rice vinegar
80 ml (⅓ cup) tomato sauce (ketchup)
300 g (1½ cups) sugar
oil, for deep-frying

Serves 4

Cut the pork into 2 cm (¾ in) cubes and put it in a bowl with the egg, 75 g (⅔ cup) of the cornflour and 2 teaspoons water. Stir to coat all pieces of pork.

Heat a wok over high heat, add the oil and heat until very hot. Stir-fry the onion for 1 minute. Add the capsicum and spring onion and cook for 1 minute. Add the pickles and toss together to combine. Add the rice vinegar, tomato sauce and sugar and stir over low heat until the sugar dissolves. Bring to the boil, then simmer for 3 minutes.

Combine the remaining cornflour with 75 ml (⅓ cup) water, add to the sweet-and-sour mixture and simmer until thickened. Set aside.

Fill a wok to one-quarter full of oil. Heat the oil to 180°C (350°F/Gas 4), or until a piece of bread fries golden brown in 15 seconds when dropped in the oil. Cook the pork in batches until it is golden brown and crispy. Return all of the pork to the wok, cook until crisp again, then remove with a wire sieve or slotted spoon and drain well. Add the pork pieces to the sauce, stir to coat, and reheat until bubbling.

sweet-and-sour pork

barbecue spareribs

1.5 kg (3 lb 5 oz) Chinese-style
   pork spareribs

MARINADE
125 ml (½ cup) hoisin sauce
3 tablespoons light soy sauce
3 tablespoons Shaoxing rice wine
2 tablespoons sugar
3 tablespoons tomato sauce (ketchup)
4 garlic cloves, finely chopped
3 tablespoons finely chopped ginger

Serves 6

Ask the butcher to cut the slab of spareribs crosswise into thirds that measure 4–5 cm (1½–2 in) in length, or use a cleaver to do so yourself.

Place the spareribs in a large clay pot, casserole dish or saucepan and cover with water. Bring to the boil, then reduce the heat to a simmer. Cook for 20 minutes, drain and allow the ribs to cool. Cut the ribs between the bones to separate them.

To make the marinade, combine the ingredients in a bowl. Add the ribs and toss lightly. Marinate in the fridge for at least 3 hours, or overnight.

Preheat the oven to 180°C (350°F/Gas 4). Put the ribs and marinade on a baking tray lined with foil. Bake for 45 minutes, turning once, until golden.

350 g (12 oz) rump or sirloin steak
1 tablespoon light soy sauce
80 ml (⅓ cup) Shaoxing rice wine
½ teaspoon roasted sesame oil
250 g (9 oz) Chinese cabbage, stems
   removed and leaves cut into
   5 cm (2 in) squares
1 tablespoon oil
2 garlic cloves, smashed with the
   flat side of a cleaver
750 ml (3 cups) chicken stock or
   recipe page 249
½ teaspoon salt
30 g (1 oz) bean thread noodles
225 g (8 oz) Chinese mushrooms (shiitake)
180 g (4 handfuls) baby spinach

DIPPING SAUCE
2 tablespoons light soy sauce
1 tablespoon Shaoxing rice wine
1 teaspoon Chinese black rice vinegar
1 teaspoon sugar
½ teaspoon chilli sauce or recipe page 250
   or dried chilli flakes (optional)
½ spring onion (scallion), finely chopped
1 teaspoon finely chopped ginger
1 garlic clove, finely chopped

Serves 6

Cut the beef across the grain into paper-thin slices. Place in a bowl and add the soy sauce, 1 tablespoon of the rice wine and the sesame oil, toss, and arrange on a platter. Separate the hard cabbage pieces from the leafy ones. Heat a wok over high heat, add the oil and heat until very hot. Stir-fry the hard cabbage and garlic for several minutes, adding 1 tablespoon of water. Add the leafy cabbage and stir-fry for several minutes. Add the rice wine, chicken stock and salt, and bring to the boil. Reduce the heat and simmer for 20 minutes.

Soak the bean thread noodles in hot water for 10 minutes, then drain and cut into 15 cm (6 in) lengths. Arrange the mushrooms, spinach and noodles on several platters and place on a table where a heated Mongolian hotpot has been set up. (If you do not have a Mongolian hotpot, use a pot and a hot plate, or an electric frying pan or an electric wok.)

Combine the dipping sauce ingredients and divide among six bowls. Pour the cabbage soup mixture into the hotpot and bring to the boil. To eat, each diner takes a slice of meat, dips it into the hot stock until the meat is cooked, then dips the meat into the dipping sauce, and eats. The mushrooms, noodles and spinach are cooked in the same way and dipped in the sauce before eating. Supply small wire strainers to cook the noodles so they stay together. The noodles and mushrooms should cook for 5–6 minutes, but the spinach should only take about 1 minute. Once all the ingredients have been eaten, the soup is eaten.

mongolian hotpot

hotpot

The great nomadic tribes of Mongolia may have ruled China for a century but, perhaps unsurprisingly, they did not leave behind a particularly impressive culinary legacy. However, one dish that did catch the imagination of the Chinese, and later all of Asia, was the Mongolian Hotpot. For the Mongolians, this was campsite food: mutton slices dunked into a pot of boiling water, fished out and eaten.

Today, every region seems to have created its own version of the hotpot, appealing to the Chinese love of combining food, friends and family. Diners sit around tall, charcoal-burning firepots that keep the broth hot. Meat, chicken, seafood, vegetables or tofu can all be added to the broth, though many versions pay homage to the original with a platter of thinly sliced lamb. Extras might include dips for the meat and bundles of noodles, which are added to the stock at the end, then drunk as a soup. Hotpot is particularly popular in China's North, where mutton is seen as a good winter tonic, in the South, where the hotpots are lighter and often medicinal, and in Sichuan, in the West, where peppery Chongqing broth is so chilli-hot that it gives off a hazy steam.

crispy shredded beef

400 g (14 oz) rump or sirloin steak,
    trimmed
2 eggs, beaten
½ teaspoon salt
4 tablespoons cornflour (cornstarch)
oil, for deep-frying
2 carrots, finely shredded
2 spring onions (scallions), shredded
1 garlic clove, finely chopped
2 red chillies, shredded
4 tablespoons caster (superfine) sugar
3 tablespoons Chinese black rice vinegar
2 tablespoons light soy sauce

Serves 4

Cut the beef into thin shreds. Combine the eggs, salt and cornflour, then coat the shredded beef with the batter. Mix well.

Fill a wok to one-quarter full of oil. Heat the oil to 180°C (350°F/Gas 4), or until a piece of bread fries golden brown in 15 seconds when dropped in the oil. Cook the beef for 3–4 minutes, stirring to separate, then remove and drain. Cook the carrot for 1½ minutes, then remove and drain. Pour the oil from the wok, leaving 1 tablespoon.

Reheat the reserved oil over high heat until very hot and stir-fry the spring onion, garlic and chilli for a few seconds. Add the beef, carrot, sugar, vinegar and soy, and stir to combine.

125 g (5 oz) cooked prawns (shrimp)
155 g (1 cup) fresh or frozen peas
1 tablespoon oil
3 spring onions (scallions), finely chopped
1 tablespoon finely chopped ginger
2 eggs, lightly beaten
1 quantity cooked rice
1½ tablespoons chicken stock or
   recipe page 249
1 tablespoon Shaoxing rice wine

2 teaspoons light soy sauce
½ teaspoon salt, or to taste
½ teaspoon roasted sesame oil
¼ teaspoon freshly ground black pepper

BOILED OR STEAMED RICE
200 g (1 cup) white long-grain rice

Serves 4

Peel the prawns, then cut in half through the back, removing the vein. Cook peas in a pan of simmering water for 3–4 minutes for fresh or 1 minute for frozen.

Heat a wok over high heat, add the oil and heat until hot. Stir-fry the spring onions and ginger for 1 minute. Reduce the heat, add the egg and lightly scramble. Add the prawns and peas and toss lightly to heat through, then add the rice before the egg is set too hard. Increase the heat and stir to separate the rice grains and break the egg into small bits. Add the stock, rice wine, soy sauce, salt, sesame oil and pepper, and toss lightly.

To make a quantity of cooked rice (four servings), place the rice in a bowl and, using your fingers as a rake, rinse under cold running water to remove any dust. Drain the rice in a colander.

To boil rice, put the rice and 420 ml (1¾ cups) water in a heavy-based pan and bring to the boil. Reduce the heat and simmer, covered, for 15–18 minutes, or until the water has evaporated and craters appear on the surface.

To steam rice, spread the rice in a steamer lined with greaseproof paper punched with holes, damp cheesecloth or muslin. Cover and steam over simmering water in a wok for 35–40 minutes, or until tender.

Fluff the rice with a fork to separate the grains. Serve or use as directed.

yangzhou fried rice with prawns

crispy noodles with beef

275 g (10 oz) fresh or 175 g (6 oz)
   dried egg noodles
1½ teaspoons roasted sesame oil
350 g (12 oz) rump or sirloin steak
1 tablespoon dark soy sauce
2 teaspoons Shaoxing rice wine
½ teaspoon sugar
1 garlic clove, finely chopped
1 teaspoon cornflour (cornstarch)
100 g (1 cup) snowpeas (mangetout),
   ends trimmed
3 tablespoons oil

SAUCE
1 tablespoon finely chopped ginger
1 spring onion (scallion), finely chopped
325 ml (1⅓ cups) chicken stock or
   recipe page 249
3 tablespoons oyster sauce
1 tablespoon Shaoxing rice wine
½ teaspoon dark soy sauce
1 teaspoon sugar
½ teaspoon roasted sesame oil
1½ tablespoons cornflour (cornstarch)

Serves 4

Cook the noodles in a pan of salted boiling water for 2–3 minutes if fresh and 10 minutes if dried, then drain and combine with 1 teaspoon of the sesame oil. Place the noodles in 4 small cake tins or flat-bottomed bowls and leave to cool.

Cut the beef across the grain into 2 mm- (⅛ in-) thick slices, then cut into 4 cm (1½ in) squares. Combine the beef, soy sauce, rice wine, sugar, garlic, cornflour and remaining sesame oil and toss. Marinate in the fridge for at least 1 hour.

Blanch the snowpeas in a pan of boiling water for 15 seconds. Drain and refresh immediately in cold water. Dry thoroughly.

Heat a wok over high heat, add 2 tablespoons of the oil and heat until almost smoking. Invert the noodle cakes, one at a time, into the wok and fry on both sides until golden, swirling the pan occasionally so the noodles cook evenly. Put the noodles on a plate and keep warm in a low oven. Reheat the wok over high heat, add the remaining oil and heat until very hot. Drain the beef and stir-fry in batches for 1 minute, or until the beef changes colour. Remove with a slotted spoon, and drain. Pour the oil from the wok, leaving 2 tablespoons.

To make the sauce, reheat the reserved oil over high heat until very hot and stir-fry the ginger and spring onion for 10 seconds, or until fragrant. Add the remaining sauce ingredients, except the cornflour, and bring to the boil. Combine the cornflour with enough water to make a paste, add to the sauce and simmer until thickened. Add the beef and snowpeas, toss to coat with the sauce, and pour the mixture over the noodles.

125 g (5 oz) minced pork or beef
½ teaspoon light soy sauce
½ teaspoon Shaoxing rice wine
½ teaspoon roasted sesame oil
125 g (5 oz) bean thread noodles
1 tablespoon oil
2 spring onions (scallions), finely chopped
1 tablespoon finely chopped ginger
1 garlic clove, finely chopped
1 teaspoon chilli bean paste
   (toban jiang), or to taste
2 spring onions (scallions), green part
   only, finely chopped

SAUCE
1 tablespoon light soy sauce
1 tablespoon Shaoxing rice wine
½ teaspoon salt
½ teaspoon sugar
½ teaspoon roasted sesame oil
250 ml (1 cup) chicken stock or
   recipe page 249

Serves 4

Combine the minced meat with the soy sauce, rice wine and sesame oil. Soak the bean thread noodles in hot water for 10 minutes, then drain.

Heat a wok over high heat, add the oil and heat until very hot. Stir-fry the minced meat, mashing and separating it, until it changes colour and starts to brown. Push the meat to the side of the wok, add the spring onions, ginger, garlic and chilli paste and stir-fry for 5 seconds, or until fragrant. Return the meat to the centre of the pan.

To make the sauce, combine all the ingredients. Add the sauce to the meat mixture and toss lightly. Add the noodles and bring to the boil. Reduce the heat to low and cook for 8 minutes, or until almost all of the liquid has evaporated. Sprinkle with the spring onions.

ants climbing trees

steamed chicken and sausage rice

4 dried Chinese mushrooms
250 g (9 oz) skinless chicken thigh fillet
1 teaspoon Shaoxing rice wine
2 teaspoons cornflour (cornstarch)
3 Chinese sausages (lap cheong)
200 g (1 cup) long-grain rice
1 spring onion (scallion), chopped

SAUCE
2 tablespoons light soy sauce
1 tablespoon Shaoxing rice wine
½ teaspoon caster (superfine) sugar
½ garlic clove, chopped (optional)
½ teaspoon chopped ginger
½ teaspoon roasted sesame oil

Serves 4

Soak the dried mushrooms in boiling water for 30 minutes, then drain and squeeze out excess water. Remove and discard the stems and shred the caps.

Cut the chicken into bite-size pieces and combine with a pinch of salt, the rice wine and cornflour.

Place the sausages on a plate in a steamer. Cover and steam over simmering water in a wok for 10 minutes, then thinly slice on the diagonal.

Put the rice in a bowl and, using your fingers as a rake, rinse under cold running water to remove any dust. Drain the rice in a colander. Place in a large clay pot or casserole dish or four individual clay pots and add enough water so there is 2 cm (¾ in) of water above the surface of the rice. Bring the water slowly to the boil, stir, then place the chicken pieces and mushrooms on top of the rice, with the sausage slices on top of them. Cook, covered, over very low heat for 15–18 minutes, or until the rice is cooked.

To make the sauce, combine the soy sauce, rice wine, sugar, garlic, ginger and sesame oil in a small saucepan and heat until almost boiling. Pour the sauce over the chicken and sausage and garnish with the spring onion.

1 teaspoon oil
10 spring onions (scallions), cut into
    4 cm (1½ in) lengths, lightly smashed
    with the flat side of a cleaver
10 garlic cloves, thinly sliced
6 slices ginger, smashed with
    the flat side of a cleaver
1½ teaspoons chilli bean paste
    (toban jiang)
2 cassia or cinnamon sticks
2 star anise
125 ml (½ cup) light soy sauce
1 kg (2 lb 4 oz) chuck steak, trimmed
    and cut into 4 cm (1½ in) cubes
250 g (9 oz) rice stick noodles
250 g (½ bunch) baby spinach
3 tablespoons finely chopped spring
    onion (scallion)

Serves 6

Heat a wok over medium heat, add the oil and heat until hot. Stir-fry the spring onions, garlic, ginger, chilli paste, cassia and star anise for 10 seconds, or until fragrant. Transfer to a clay pot, casserole dish or saucepan. Add the soy sauce and 2.25 litres (8 cups) water. Bring to the boil, add the beef, then return to the boil. Reduce the heat and simmer, covered, for 1½ hours, or until the beef is very tender. Skim the surface occasionally to remove impurities and fat. Remove and discard the ginger and cassia.

Soak the noodles in hot water for 10 minutes, then drain and divide among six bowls. Add the spinach to the beef and bring to the boil.

Spoon the beef mixture over the noodles and sprinkle with the spring onion.

cinnamon beef noodles

发展创造

fried fragrant bananas

125 g (1 cup) self-raising flour
2 tablespoons milk
20 g (1 tablespoon) butter, melted
1 tablespoon caster (superfine) sugar
4 apple or lady finger bananas, or
**   3 ordinary bananas**
oil, for deep-frying
honey (optional)

Serves 4

Combine the flour, milk, butter and sugar, then add enough water to make a thick batter.

Cut the bananas into 3 cm (1 in) chunks.

Fill a wok to one-quarter full of oil. Heat the oil to 180°C (350°F/Gas 4), or until a piece of bread fries golden brown in 15 seconds when dropped in the oil. Dip the banana pieces, a few at a time, into the batter, then fry them for 3 minutes, or until they are well browned on all sides. Drain the banana pieces on paper towels.

Serve the bananas drizzled with honey for extra sweetness.

200 g (1 cup) young ginger
1 tablespoon sugar
500 ml (2 cups) milk

Serves 4

Grate the ginger as finely as you can, collecting any juice. Place the grated ginger in a piece of muslin, twist the top hard and squeeze out as much juice as possible. You will need 4 tablespoons. Alternatively, you can push the ginger through a juicer.

Put 1 tablespoon of ginger juice and 1 teaspoon of sugar each into four bowls. Put the milk in a saucepan and bring to the boil, then divide among the bowls. Leave to set for 1 minute (the ginger juice will cause the milk to solidify). Serve warm.

ginger pudding

a little taste of...

A Chinese banquet is all about conspicuous consumption. Often a huge affair, rarely held at home, it can celebrate a birthday, wedding, festival, even a funeral. Banquets are also an essential part of building close working relationships, though food, not business, is always the main topic at the table. The meal consists of at least eight to 12 dishes, brought out one by one to be exclaimed over. This is by no means everyday fare, each dish must be special, and special often means expensive — abalone, lobster, shark's fin, a whole fish or roast duck. Plain rice and noodles are served at the end, but it is polite to leave them untouched. Etiquette is important at these events, and the seating plan reflects a strict pecking order. The host's duties include providing alcohol for each table, preferably a bottle of Cognac, a status symbol that guests pour freely for each other. He will also urge the guests of honour to take the choicest food, such as the fish's head, sometimes even placing the tastiest morsels in the guests' bowls himself. Once the fruit has been served, it's time to leave, because at a banquet, there's no lingering when the food is gone.

...banquet food

candied walnuts

250 g (1 cup) sugar
450 g (5 cups) shelled walnut halves
oil, for deep-frying

Serves 8 as a snack

Dissolve the sugar in 100 ml (½ cup) water, then bring to the boil and cook for 2 minutes.

Blanch the walnuts in a pan of boiling water briefly, then drain. Tip the walnuts immediately into the syrup, stirring to coat. Cool for 5 minutes, then drain.

Fill a wok to one-quarter full of oil. Heat the oil to 190°C (375°F/Gas 5), or until a piece of bread fries golden brown in 10 seconds when dropped in the oil. Add the walnuts in batches, stirring to brown evenly. As soon as they brown, remove with a wire sieve or slotted spoon and put on some foil, making sure they are well spaced. Do not touch as they will be hot. When cool, drain on paper towels. Serve as a snack or at the start of a meal.

300 g (11 oz) ready-prepared
  shark's fin
400 g (14 oz) bacon or ham bones
500 g (1lb 2 oz) chicken bones
500 g (1 lb 2 oz) beef bones
4 slices ginger
300 g (11 oz) skinless chicken breast
  fillet, minced

1 egg white, lightly beaten
4 tablespoons cornflour (cornstarch)
1 tablespoon light soy sauce
red rice vinegar

Serves 6

Place the shark's fin in a large bowl and cover with cold water. Leave to soak overnight. Strain the shark's fin and rinse gently to remove any remaining sand and sediment. Bring a stockpot of water to the boil. Add the shark's fin, reduce the heat and simmer, covered, for 1 hour. Strain and set aside.

Place the bacon or ham bones, chicken bones and beef bones in a large stockpot with the ginger slices and 2 litres (8 cups) water. Bring to the boil, then reduce the heat and simmer, covered, for 2 hours. Skim off any scum and fat during cooking. Strain the stock, discarding the bones. Measure the stock; you will need 1.5–1.75 litres (6–7 cups). If you have more, return the stock to the pan and reduce it further until you have the correct amount.

Combine the chicken, egg white and 1 tablespoon of the cornflour. Set aside in the fridge.

Put the prepared shark's fin and stock in a large clay pot or saucepan and simmer, covered, for 30 minutes. Add the chicken mixture and stir to separate the meat. Simmer for 10 minutes, or until the chicken is cooked.

Season the soup with the soy sauce and some salt and white pepper. Combine the remaining cornflour with 125 ml (½ cup) water, add to the soup and simmer until thickened.

Serve the soup with some red rice vinegar, which can be added to the soup to taste.

shark's fin soup

abalone, snowpeas and oyster mushrooms

1.3 kg (3 lb) fresh abalone or 450 g (1 lb)
    prepared weight or 450 g (1 lb)
    tinned abalone
300 g (3 cups) snowpeas (mangetout),
    ends trimmed
150 g (6 oz) oyster mushrooms
2 tablespoons oil
2 garlic cloves, finely chopped

2 teaspoons finely chopped ginger
2 tablespoons oyster sauce
2 teaspoons light soy sauce
1 teaspoon sugar
3 teaspoons cornflour (cornstarch)

Serves 4

Prepare the fresh abalone by removing the meat from the shell using a sharp knife. Wash the meat under cold running water, rubbing well to remove any dark-coloured slime. Trim off any hard outer edges and the mouth as well as any hard patches on the bottom of the foot. Pound the meat with a mallet for 1 minute to tenderize it, but be careful not to break the flesh.

Place the fresh abalone in a saucepan of simmering water and cook, covered, for about 2 hours, or until the meat is tender (test it by seeing if a fork will pierce the meat easily). Drain the abalone and, when it is cool enough to handle, cut it into thin slices.

If you are using tinned abalone, simply drain, reserving the juice, and cut into thin slices.

Cut any large snowpeas in half diagonally. Halve any large oyster mushrooms.

Heat a wok over medium heat, add the oil and heat until hot. Stir-fry the snowpeas and mushrooms for 1 minute. Add the garlic and ginger and stir for 1 minute, or until aromatic.

Reduce the heat slightly and add the oyster sauce, soy sauce, sugar and the sliced abalone. Stir well to combine. Combine the cornflour with enough water (or the reserved abalone juice if using tinned abalone) to make a paste, add to the sauce and simmer until thickened.

350 g (12 oz) scallops, roe removed
2 tablespoons Shaoxing rice wine
1 tablespoon roasted sesame oil
1 teaspoon finely chopped ginger
½ spring onion (scallion), finely chopped
200 g (7 oz) Chinese broccoli (gai lan) or
   bok choy (pak choi)
80 ml (⅓ cup) chicken stock or
   recipe page 249
½ teaspoon salt

¼ teaspoon sugar
¼ teaspoon freshly ground white pepper
1 teaspoon cornflour (cornstarch)
1 tablespoon oil
1 tablespoon finely shredded ginger
1 spring onion (scallion), finely shredded
1 garlic clove, very thinly sliced

Serves 6

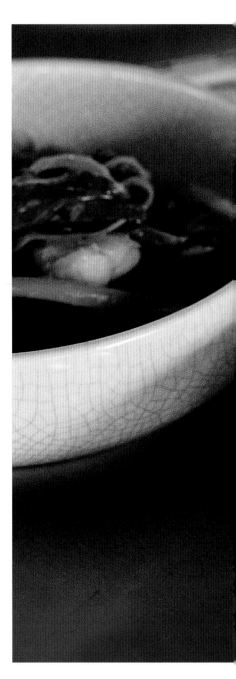

Slice the small, hard white muscle off the side of each scallop and pull off any membrane. Rinse the scallops and drain. Holding a knife blade parallel to the cutting surface, slice each scallop in half horizontally. Place the scallops in a bowl with 1 tablespoon of the rice wine, ¼ teaspoon of the sesame oil and the chopped ginger and spring onion. Toss lightly, then leave to marinate for 20 minutes.

Wash the broccoli well. Discard any tough-looking stems and diagonally cut into 2 cm (¾ in) pieces through the stem and the leaf. Blanch the broccoli in a pan of boiling water for 2 minutes, or until the stems and leaves are just tender, then refresh in cold water and dry thoroughly.

Combine the chicken stock, salt, sugar, white pepper, cornflour and the remaining rice wine and sesame oil.

Heat a wok over high heat, add the oil and heat until very hot. Add the scallops and stir-fry for 30 seconds, then remove. Add the shredded ginger, spring onion and garlic and stir-fry for 10 seconds. Add the stock mixture and cook, stirring constantly, until the sauce thickens. Add the broccoli and scallops. Toss lightly to coat with the sauce.

stir-fried scallops

stir-fried squid

400 g (14 oz) squid tubes
3 tablespoons oil
2 tablespoons salted, fermented black
   beans, rinsed and mashed
1 small onion, cut into small cubes
1 small green capsicum (pepper),
   cut into small cubes
3–4 small slices ginger
1 spring onion (scallion),
   cut into short lengths
1 small red chilli, chopped
1 tablespoon Shaoxing rice wine
½ teaspoon roasted sesame oil

Serves 4

Open up the squid tubes and scrub off any soft jelly-like substance, then score the inside of the flesh with a fine crisscross pattern, making sure you do not cut all the way through. Cut the squid into three 5 cm- (2 in-) long pieces.

Blanch the squid in a pan of boiling water for 25–30 seconds; each piece will curl up and the crisscross pattern will open out, hence the name 'squid flower'. Remove and refresh in cold water, then drain and dry well.

Heat a wok over high heat, add the oil and heat until very hot. Stir-fry the black beans, onion, capsicum, ginger, spring onion and chilli for 1 minute. Add the squid and rice wine, mix together and stir for 1 minute. Sprinkle with the sesame oil.

600 g (1 lb 5 oz) tiger prawns
1 tablespoon cornflour (cornstarch)
½ egg white, beaten
oil, for deep-frying
150 g (6 oz) snowpeas (mangetout),
   ends trimmed
½ teaspoon salt
½ teaspoon sugar
1 spring onion (scallion), finely chopped

1 teaspoon finely chopped ginger
1 tablespoon light soy sauce
1 tablespoon Shaoxing rice wine
½ teaspoon roasted sesame oil
1 tablespoon chilli bean paste (toban jiang)
1 tablespoon tomato paste (purée)

Serves 4

Peel and devein the prawns, leaving the tails intact. Combine the cornflour with enough water to make a paste. Stir in the egg white and a pinch of salt, then stir in the prawns.

Fill a wok to one-quarter full of oil. Heat the oil to 180°C (350°F/Gas 4), or until a piece of bread fries golden brown in 15 seconds when dropped in the oil. Cook the prawns for 1 minute, stirring to separate them. Remove the prawns from the wok with a wire sieve or slotted spoon as soon as the colour changes, then drain. Pour the oil from the wok, leaving 1 tablespoon.

Reheat the reserved oil over high heat until very hot and stir-fry the snowpeas with the salt and sugar for 1½ minutes. Remove and place in the centre of a serving platter.

Reheat the wok again and stir-fry the spring onion and ginger for a few seconds. Add the prawns, soy sauce and rice wine, blend well and stir-fry for about 30 seconds, then add the sesame oil. Transfer about half of the prawns to one end of the serving platter.

Add the chilli bean paste and the tomato paste to the remaining prawns, blend well, tossing to coat the prawns, then transfer the prawns to the other end of the platter.

love birds prawns

chinese new year...

In perhaps no other civilization does food and spirituality interweave so closely. Through food the Chinese speak to their gods and ghosts, from the Hungry Ghosts and Qing Ming festivals, where roast pig, duck and pork are eaten in memory of the dead, to the oranges and tasty titbits laid out for ancestors at shrines in streets, shops and at home.

In a year defined by festivals, Chinese New Year is the biggest celebration of them all. In the days leading up to it, homes are a bustle of activity, cleaning

and clearing away all the debris of the old year, a flurry of lucky red-and-gold decorations plastered on walls and doors. Each stage of the celebrations is marked with food. At the end of the final lunar month, the home's Kitchen God is pandered to with a meal of sweets and wines before ascending to heaven for the annual feedback on his family's activities. On New Year's Eve, families

make great efforts to gather at home to celebrate together with a banquet of auspicious dishes. Every dish is symbolic, representing a hope for the year to come. The most popular wishes are happiness, wealth, longevity and fertility. Long, unbroken noodles wish a long life on guests and a vegetarian dish promises purification. A whole fish is then served at the end of the meal to signify abundance — the word for fish, *yu*, also means abundance. There should be fish left over to bring plenty in the months to come.

Banquets are all about extravagance, and a family will endeavour to excel itself with at least one special dish, such as abalone, whose Chinese name even sounds like the expression for guaranteed wealth. On New Year's Day, little red envelopes of money, *lai see*, are exchanged along with oranges lovingly wrapped in red paper, their name being similar to that for gold. Chinese New Year celebrations continue for a further two weeks, until the Lantern Festival finally marks the end with fireworks, firecrackers and tiny sweet dumplings.

chilli crab

4 x 250 g (9 oz) live crabs
3 tablespoons oil
1 tablespoon Guilin chilli sauce
2 tablespoons light soy sauce
3 teaspoons clear rice vinegar
4 tablespoons Shaoxing rice wine
½ teaspoon salt
2 tablespoons sugar

2 tablespoons chicken stock
  or recipe page 249
1 tablespoon grated ginger
2 garlic cloves, crushed
2 spring onions (scallions), finely chopped

Serves 4

To kill the crabs humanely, put them in the freezer for 1 hour. Bring a large saucepan of water to the boil. Plunge the crabs into boiling water for about 1 minute, then rinse them in cold water. Twist off and discard the upper shell, and remove and discard the spongy grey gill tissue from inside the crab. Rinse the bodies and drain well. Cut away the last two hairy joints of the legs. Cut each crab into four to six pieces, cutting so that a portion of the body is attached to one or two legs. Crack the crab claws using crab crackers or the back edge of a cleaver—this will help the flavouring penetrate the crab meat.

Heat a wok over high heat, add 1 tablespoon of the oil and heat until very hot. Add half the crab and fry for several minutes to cook the meat right through. Remove and drain. Repeat with another tablespoon of the oil and the remaining crab.

Combine the chilli sauce, soy sauce, rice vinegar, rice wine, salt, sugar and stock in a bowl.

Reheat the wok over high heat, add the remaining oil and heat until very hot. Stir-fry the ginger, garlic and spring onions for 10 seconds. Add the sauce mixture to the wok and cook briefly. Add the crab pieces and toss lightly to coat with the sauce. Cook, covered, for 5 minutes, then serve immediately.

Crab is best eaten with your hands, so supply finger bowls as well as special picks to help remove the meat from the crab claws.

3–4 dried Chinese mushrooms
750 g–1 kg (1 lb 10 oz–2 lb 4 oz) whole
 fish, such as carp, bream, grouper or
 sea bass
1 teaspoon salt
oil, for deep-frying
2 tablespoons oil, extra
1 tablespoon shredded ginger
2 spring onions (scallions), shredded
½ small carrot, shredded
½ small green capsicum (pepper),
 shredded

½ celery stalk, shredded
2 red chillies, seeded and finely shredded
2 tablespoons light soy sauce
3 tablespoons sugar
3 tablespoons Chinese black rice vinegar
1 tablespoon Shaoxing rice wine
125 ml (½ cup) chicken and meat stock
 or recipe page 249
1 tablespoon cornflour (cornstarch)
½ teaspoon roasted sesame oil

Serves 4

Soak the dried mushrooms in boiling water for 30 minutes, then drain and squeeze out excess water. Remove and discard the stems. Finely shred the caps.

If you buy a live fish, ask the fishmonger to gut it through the gills. This is harder than gutting through the stomach, but leaves the fish looking whole. If you are gutting the fish yourself, make a cut from the throat to the tail and pull out the guts through the stomach. Remove any scales with a fish scaler or the back of a knife. Check that the gills have been cut out, then rinse the fish under cold, running water and drain thoroughly in a colander. Diagonally score both sides of the fish, cutting through as far as the bone at intervals of 2 cm (¾ in). Rub salt over the inside and outside of the fish and into the slits.

Fill a wok to one-quarter full of oil. Heat the oil to 190°C (375°F/Gas 5), or until a piece of bread fries golden brown in 10 seconds when dropped in the oil. Holding the fish by its tail, gently and carefully lower it into the oil. Cook the fish for 3–4 minutes on each side, or until the fish flakes when the skin is pressed firmly or the dorsal fin pulls out easily. Remove from the wok and drain on paper towels, then place on a dish and keep warm in a low oven. Pour off the oil and wipe out the wok.

Reheat the wok over high heat, add the extra oil and heat until very hot. Stir-fry the mushrooms, ginger, spring onion, carrot, capsicum, celery and chilli for 1½ minutes. Add the soy sauce, sugar, rice vinegar, rice wine and stock, and bring to the boil. Combine the cornflour with enough water to make a paste, add to the sauce and simmer until thickened. Add the sesame oil, blend well and spoon over the fish.

shanghai-style
five-willow fish

泰式泡鳳爪

salt-baked chicken

1.5 kg chicken (3 lb 5 oz)
2 tablespoons light soy sauce
2 kg (4 lb 8 oz) sea salt or coarse salt

FILLING
1 spring onion (scallion), chopped
1 teaspoon grated ginger
2 star anise, crushed
½ teaspoon salt
4 tablespoons Mei Kuei Lu Chiew
    or brandy

DIPPING SAUCE
1 tablespoon oil
1 spring onion (scallion), chopped
1 teaspoon chopped ginger
½ teaspoon salt
50 ml (¼ cup) chicken and meat stock
    or recipe page 249

Serves 4

Rinse the chicken, drain, and remove any fat from the cavity opening and around the neck. Cut off and discard the parson's nose. Blanch the chicken in a pan of boiling water for 2–3 minutes, then refresh under cold water and dry well. Brush the chicken with the soy sauce and hang it up to dry in a cool and airy place for a couple of hours, or leave it uncovered in the fridge.

Meanwhile, to make the filling, combine the spring onion, ginger, star anise, salt and Mei Kuei Lu Chiew. Pour the filling into the cavity of the chicken. Wrap the chicken tightly with a large sheet of cheesecloth or fine muslin.

Heat the salt in a large clay pot or casserole dish very slowly until very hot, then turn off the heat and remove about half. Make a hole in the centre of the salt and place the chicken in it, breast side up, then cover with the salt removed earlier so the chicken is completely buried. Cover the clay pot and cook over medium heat for 15–20 minutes, then reduce the heat to low and cook for about 45–50 minutes. Leave for at least 15–20 minutes before taking the chicken out. (The salt can be reused.)

To make the dipping sauce, heat the oil in a small wok or saucepan. Fry the spring onion and ginger for 1 minute, then add the salt and stock. Bring to the boil, then reduce the heat and simmer for a couple of minutes.

Remove the chicken from the clay pot and unwrap it. Using a cleaver, cut the chicken through the bones into bite-size pieces. Arrange on a serving dish and serve hot or cold with the dipping sauce.

12 soft lettuce leaves, such as butter
  lettuce
250 g (9 oz) squab or pigeon breast meat
450 g (1 lb) centre-cut pork loin, trimmed
90 ml (⅓ cup) light soy sauce
3½ tablespoons Shaoxing rice wine
2½ teaspoons roasted sesame oil
8 dried Chinese mushrooms
240 g (1½ cups) peeled water chestnuts

120 ml (½ cup) oil
2 spring onions (scallions), finely chopped
2 tablespoons finely chopped ginger
1 teaspoon salt
1 teaspoon sugar
1 teaspoon cornflour (cornstarch)

Serves 6

Rinse the lettuce and separate the leaves. Drain thoroughly, then lightly pound each leaf with the flat side of a cleaver. Arrange the flattened leaves in a basket or on a platter and set aside.

Mince the squab meat in a food processor or chop very finely with a sharp knife. Mince the pork to the same size as the squab. Place the squab and pork in a bowl with 2 tablespoons of the soy sauce, 1½ tablespoons of the rice wine and 1 teaspoon of the sesame oil, and toss lightly. Marinate in the fridge for 20 minutes.

Soak the dried mushrooms in boiling water for 30 minutes, then drain and squeeze out any excess water. Remove and discard the stems and chop the caps. Blanch the water chestnuts in a pan of boiling water for 1 minute, then refresh in cold water. Drain, pat dry and roughly chop them.

Heat a wok over high heat, add 3 tablespoons of the oil and heat until very hot. Stir-fry the meat mixture, mashing and separating the pieces, until browned. Remove and drain. Reheat the wok, add 3 tablespoons more of the oil and heat until very hot. Stir-fry the spring onions and ginger, turning constantly, for 10 seconds, or until fragrant. Add the mushrooms and stir-fry for 5 seconds, turning constantly. Add the water chestnuts and stir-fry for 15 seconds, or until heated through. Add the remaining soy sauce, rice wine and sesame oil with the salt, sugar, cornflour and 125 ml (½ cup) water. Stir-fry, stirring constantly, until thickened. Add the cooked meat mixture and toss lightly.

To serve, place some of the stir-fried meat in a lettuce leaf, roll up and eat.

fried squab
in lettuce

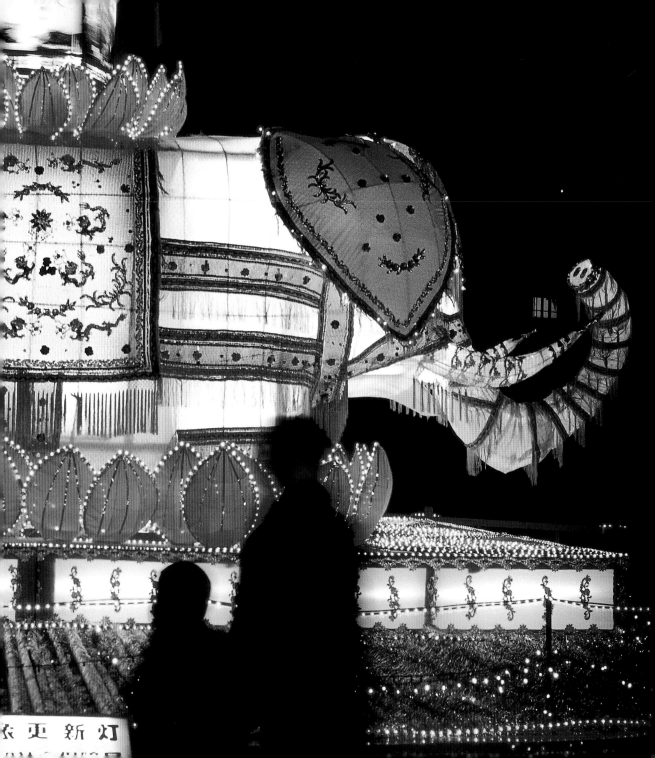

fried quails
with spicy salt

SPICY SALT AND PEPPER
1 tablespoon salt
2 teaspoons ground Sichuan peppercorns
1 teaspoon five-spice powder

Makes 2 tablespoons

4 quails
1 teaspoon spicy salt and pepper
1 teaspoon sugar
1 tablespoon light soy sauce
1 tablespoon Shaoxing rice wine
2–3 tablespoons plain (all-purpose) flour
oil, for deep-frying
1 spring onion (scallion), finely chopped
1 red chilli, finely chopped

Serves 4

To make the spicy salt and pepper, combine the salt, Sichuan peppercorns and five-spice powder. Dry-fry over low heat, stirring constantly, for 2–3 minutes, or until aromatic.

Split each quail in half down the middle and clean well. Marinate with the spicy salt and pepper, the sugar, soy sauce and rice wine for 2–3 hours in the fridge, turning frequently. Coat each quail piece in the flour.

Fill a wok to one-quarter full of oil. Heat the oil to 190°C (375°F/Gas 5), or until a piece of bread fries golden brown in 10 seconds when dropped in the oil. Reduce the heat and fry the quail for 2–3 minutes on each side. Remove from the wok and drain on paper towels.

Soak the spring onion and chilli in the hot oil (with the heat turned off) for 2 minutes. Remove with a wire sieve or slotted spoon and drain, then sprinkle over the quail pieces. Serve hot.

2.25 kg (5 lb) duck
2 teaspoons salt
4 spring onions (scallions),
    each tied in a knot
4 x 1 cm (¼ in) slices ginger, smashed
    with the flat side of a cleaver
6 star anise
3 cinnamon or cassia sticks
1 tablespoon Sichuan peppercorns
100 ml (⅓ cup) Shaoxing rice wine
200 ml (⅔ cup) light soy sauce
100 ml (⅓ cup) dark soy sauce
100 g (4 oz) rock (lump) sugar

Serves 4

Rinse the duck, drain, and remove any fat from the cavity opening and around the neck. Cut off and discard the parson's nose. Blanch the duck in a pan of boiling water for 2–3 minutes, then refresh in cold water. Pat dry and rub the salt inside the cavity.

Place the duck, breast-side-up, in a clay pot or casserole dish, and add the spring onion, ginger, star anise, cinnamon, peppercorns, rice wine, soy sauces, rock sugar and enough water to cover. Bring to the boil, then reduce the heat and simmer, covered, for 40–45 minutes. Turn off the heat and leave the duck to cool in the liquid for 2–3 hours, transferring the clay pot to the fridge once it is cool enough. Leave in the fridge until completely cold (you can keep the duck in the liquid overnight and serve it the next day).

To serve, remove the duck from the liquid and drain well. Using a cleaver, cut the duck through the bones into bite-size pieces.

Traditionally, this dish is served at room temperature, but if you would like to serve it hot, put the clay pot with the duck and the liquid back on the stove and bring it to the boil. Simmer for 10 minutes, or until the duck is completely heated through.

The sauce can be reused as a master sauce (see page 253).

shanghai soy duck

peking duck

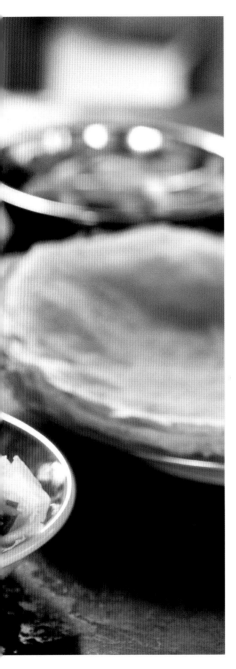

2.5 kg (5 lb 8 oz) duck
2 tablespoons maltose or honey, dissolved
in 2 tablespoons water
125 ml (½ cup) hoisin sauce or plum sauce
24 Mandarin pancakes (page 248)
6–8 spring onions (scallions), shredded
½ cucumber, shredded

Serves 6

Cut the wing tips off the duck with a pair of poultry shears. Rinse the duck, drain, and remove any fat from the cavity opening and around the neck. Cut off and discard the parson's nose. Plunge the duck into a pot of boiling water for 2–3 minutes to tighten the skin. Remove and drain, then dry thoroughly.

While the skin is still warm, brush the duck all over with the maltose and water solution, then hang it up to dry in a cool and airy place for at least 6 hours, or overnight, or leave it uncovered in the fridge.

Preheat the oven to 200°C (400°F/Gas 6). Place the duck, breast-side-up, on a rack in a roasting tin, and cook without basting or turning for 1½ hours. Check to make sure the duck is not getting too dark and, if it is, cover it loosely with foil.

To serve, remove the crispy duck skin in small slices by using a sharp carving knife, then carve the meat, or carve both together. Arrange on a serving plate.

To eat, spread about 1 teaspoon of the hoisin sauce or plum sauce in the centre of a pancake, add a few strips of spring onion, cucumber, duck skin and meat, then roll up the pancake. Turn up the bottom edge to prevent the contents from falling out.

peking duck

Peking Duck is one of the stars of the Chinese culinary repertoire and its appeal is universal: a contrast of crisp, dark red duck skin wrapped in the softest pancakes, a bite of spring onion and touch of sweet bean paste. Peking Duck has always been essentially a restaurant dish, not just because of the red-hot wood-fired ovens needed to make it, but also because, unlike most other Chinese dishes, this one is not simply placed on the table ready to eat. Probably a relatively recent reaction to its growing popularity, it is instead served with a rare

touch of showbiz. Staff wheel the prepared duck out of the kitchen on a trolley. They then delicately carve the skin and meat with a cleaver at the table.

Peking Duck was almost certainly concocted in the emperors' kitchens and makes clever use of the region's ducks, the method of preparation melting away the bird's high proportion of fat while the skin crisps. Many of the city's best-known restaurants are multi-level temples specialising in duck, where diners can order not just the main event, but a duck banquet, eating literally from beak to feet.

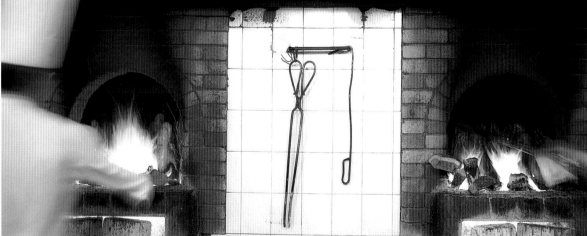

mu shu pork

250 g (9 oz) centre-cut pork loin, trimmed
55 ml (¼ cup) light soy sauce
50 ml (¼ cup) Shaoxing rice wine
½ teaspoon roasted sesame oil
2 teaspoons cornflour (cornstarch)
5 dried Chinese mushrooms
20 g (1 oz) dried black fungus (wood ears)
4 tablespoons oil
2 eggs, lightly beaten
4 garlic cloves, finely chopped

2 tablespoons finely chopped ginger
1 leek, white part only, finely shredded
¼ small Chinese cabbage, shredded, stem
   sections and leafy sections separated
½ teaspoon sugar
¼ teaspoon freshly ground black pepper
75 ml (⅓ cup) hoisin sauce
12 Mandarin pancakes (page 248)

Serves 4

Cut the pork across the grain into slices about 5 mm (¼ in) thick, then cut into thin, matchstick-size shreds about 2 cm (¾ in) long. Put the shreds in a bowl, add 1 tablespoon of the soy sauce, 1 tablespoon of the rice wine, the sesame oil and 1 teaspoon of the cornflour, and toss lightly to coat. Cover with plastic wrap and marinate in the fridge for 30 minutes.

Soak the dried mushrooms in boiling water for 30 minutes, then drain and squeeze out any excess water. Remove and discard the stems and shred the caps. Soak the fungus in cold water for 20 minutes, then drain and squeeze out any excess water. Shred the fungus.

Heat a wok over high heat, add 2 tablespoons of the oil and heat until very hot. Stir-fry the pork mixture for 2–3 minutes, until the meat is brown and cooked. Remove with a wire sieve or slotted spoon and drain. Rinse out and dry the wok.

Reheat the wok over high heat, add 1 tablespoon of the oil and heat until hot. Stir-fry the eggs to scramble, then move to the side of the wok. Add 1 tablespoon of the oil, heat until very hot, and stir-fry the garlic, ginger, mushrooms and fungus for 10 seconds, or until fragrant. Add the leek and toss lightly for 1½ minutes, then add the cabbage stems and stir-fry for 30 seconds. Add the leafy cabbage sections, and cook for 1 minute, or until the vegetables are just tender. Combine 1½ tablespoons of the soy sauce, the remaining rice wine and cornflour, the sugar, black pepper and the meat, add to the sauce and simmer until thickened.

Combine the hoisin sauce, remaining soy sauce and 1½ tablespoons water in a small bowl. Serve the pork with the pancakes and sauce.

300 g (11 oz) lamb fillet
2 teaspoons finely chopped ginger
1 spring onion (scallion), chopped
2 teaspoons ground Sichuan peppercorns
1 teaspoon salt
2 tablespoons light soy sauce
1 tablespoon yellow bean sauce
1 tablespoon hoisin sauce
1 teaspoon five-spice powder
2 tablespoons Shaoxing rice wine
oil, for deep-frying
crisp lettuce leaves
100 ml (⅓ cup) hoisin sauce, extra
½ cucumber, shredded
6 spring onions (scallions), shredded

Serves 4

Cut the lamb along the grain into six long strips. Combine with the ginger, spring onions, pepper, salt, soy, yellow bean and hoisin sauces, five-spice powder and rice wine. Marinate in the fridge for at least 2 hours. Put the lamb and marinade in a heatproof dish in a steamer. Cover and steam for 2½–3 hours over simmering water in a wok, replenishing with boiling water during cooking. Remove the lamb from the liquid and drain well.

Fill a wok to one-quarter full of oil. Heat the oil to 180°C (350°F/Gas 4), or until a piece of bread fries golden brown in 15 seconds when dropped in the oil. Cook the lamb for 3–4 minutes, then remove and drain. Cut the lamb into bite-size shreds.

To serve, place some lamb in the lettuce leaves with some hoisin sauce, cucumber and spring onion and roll up into a parcel.

mongolian lamb

beef with oyster sauce

300 g (11 oz) rump or sirloin steak,
  trimmed
1 teaspoon sugar
1 tablespoon dark soy sauce
2 teaspoons Shaoxing rice wine
2 teaspoons cornflour (cornstarch)
4 dried Chinese mushrooms
oil, for deep-frying
4 slices ginger
1 spring onion (scallion), cut into
  short lengths
75 g (3 oz) snowpeas (mangetout),
  ends trimmed
1 small carrot, thinly sliced
½ teaspoon salt
2–3 tablespoons chicken and meat stock
  or recipe page 249
2 tablespoons oyster sauce

Serves 4

Cut the beef across the grain into thin bite-size slices. Combine with half the sugar, the soy sauce, rice wine, cornflour and 2 tablespoons water. Marinate in the fridge for several hours, or overnight.

Soak the dried mushrooms in boiling water for 30 minutes, then drain and squeeze out any excess water. Remove and discard the stems and cut the caps in half, or quarters if large.

Fill a wok to one-quarter full of oil. Heat the oil to 180°C (350°F/Gas 4), or until a piece of bread fries golden brown in 15 seconds when dropped in the oil. Cook the beef for 45–50 seconds, stirring to separate the pieces, and remove as soon as the colour changes. Drain well in a colander. Pour the oil from the wok, leaving 2 tablespoons.

Reheat the reserved oil over high heat until very hot and stir-fry the ginger and spring onion for 1 minute. Add the snowpeas, mushrooms and carrot and stir-fry for 1 minute, then add the salt, stock and remaining sugar and stir-fry for 1 minute. Toss with the beef and the oyster sauce.

250 g (9 oz) precooked longevity
   or dried egg noodles
100 g (1 cup) bean sprouts
100 g (⅓ cup) fresh or tinned bamboo
   shoots, rinsed and drained
1 tablespoon oil
1 tablespoon finely chopped ginger
4 spring onions (scallions), thinly sliced
1 tablespoon light soy sauce
1 teaspoon roasted sesame oil
75 ml (⅓ cup) chicken stock or
   recipe page 249

Serves 4

If using longevity noodles, cook in a pan of salted boiling water for 1 minute, drain, then rinse in cold water. If using dried egg noodles, cook in a pan of salted boiling water for 10 minutes, then drain. Wash the bean sprouts and drain thoroughly. Shred the bamboo shoots.

Heat a wok over high heat, add the oil and heat until very hot. Stir-fry the ginger for a few seconds, then add the bean sprouts, bamboo shoots and spring onions and stir-fry for 1 minute. Add the soy sauce, sesame oil and stock and bring to the boil. Add the longevity or dried egg noodles and toss together until the sauce is absorbed.

longevity noodles

eight-treasure rice

12 whole blanched lotus seeds
12 jujubes (dried Chinese dates)
20 fresh or tinned ginkgo nuts, shelled
225 g (1 cup) glutinous rice
2 tablespoons sugar
2 teaspoons oil
30 g (1 oz) brown sugar
8 glacé cherries
6 dried longans, pitted
4 almonds or walnuts
225 g (8 oz) red bean paste

Serves 8

Soak the lotus seeds and jujubes in bowls of cold water for 30 minutes, then drain. Remove the seeds from the jujubes. If using fresh ginkgo nuts, blanch in c pan of boiling water for 5 minutes, then refresh in cold water and dry thoroughly.

Put the glutinous rice and 300 ml (1¼ cups) water in a heavy-based saucepan and bring to the boil. Reduce the heat to low and simmer for 10–15 minutes. Stir in the sugar and oil.

Dissolve the sugar in 200 ml (¾ cup) water and bring to the boil. Add the lotus seeds, jujubes and ginkgo nuts and simmer for 1 hour, or until the lotus seeds are soft. Drain, reserving the liquid.

Grease a 1 litre (4 cup) heatproof bowl and decorate the base with the lotus seeds, jujubes, ginkgo nuts, cherries, longans and almonds. Smooth two-thirds of the rice over this to form a shell on the surface of the bowl. Fill with the bean paste, cover with the remaining rice and smooth the surface.

Cover the rice with a piece of greased foil and put the bowl in a steamer. Cover and steam over simmering water in a wok for 1–1½ hours, replenishing with boiling water during cooking.

Turn out the pudding onto a plate and pour the reserved sugar liquid over the top. Serve hot.

**60 g (2½ oz) black sesame paste, red
   bean paste or smooth peanut butter**
4 tablespoons caster (superfine) sugar
250 g (1½ cups) glutinous rice flour
30 g (1 oz) rock (lump) sugar

Makes 24

Combine the sesame paste with the caster sugar.

Sift the rice flour into a bowl and stir in 200 ml (¾ cup) boiling water. Knead carefully (the dough will be very hot) to form a soft, slightly sticky dough. Dust your hands with extra rice flour, roll the dough into a cylinder, then divide it into cherry-size pieces. Cover the dough with a tea towel and, using one piece at a time, form each piece of dough into a flat round, then gather it into a cup shape. The dough should be fairly thin.

Fill each cup shape with 1 teaspoon of paste and fold the top over, smoothing the dough so you have a round ball with no visible joins.

Bring 1 litre water to the boil, add the rock sugar and stir until dissolved. Return to the boil, add the dumplings in batches and simmer for 5 minutes, or until they rise to the surface. Serve warm with a little of the syrup.

new year
sweet dumplings

almond tofu with fruit

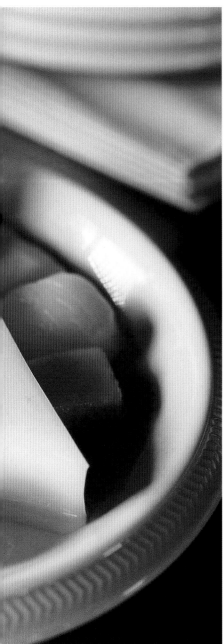

2½ tablespoons powdered gelatine or
   6 gelatine sheets
90 g (⅓ cup) caster (superfine) sugar
2 teaspoons almond extract
125 ml (½ cup) condensed milk
400 g (14 oz) tin lychees in syrup
400 g (14 oz) tin loquats in syrup
½ papaya, cut into cubes
½ melon, cut into cubes

Serves 6

Put 125 ml (½ cup) water in a saucepan. If you are using powdered gelatine, sprinkle it on the water and leave to sponge for 1 minute. If you are using gelatine sheets, soak in the water until floppy. Heat the mixture slightly, stirring constantly to dissolve the gelatine.

Place the sugar, almond extract and condensed milk in a bowl and stir to combine. Slowly add 625 ml (2½ cups) water, stirring to dissolve the sugar. Stir in the dissolved gelatine. Pour into a chilled 23 cm (9 in) square tin. Chill for at least 4 hours, or until set.

Drain half the syrup from the lychees and the loquats. Place the lychees and loquats with their remaining syrup in a large bowl. Add the cubed papaya and melon. Cut the almond tofu into diamond-shaped pieces and arrange on plates, then spoon the fruit around the tofu.

a little taste...

Wet markets are China's food stores, where local farmers congregate to sell their goods. Found rambling through city streets or inside purpose-built market halls, Chinese cooks will visit their local market at least once a day, ensuring that they grab the best ingredients and the latest gossip. The market is divided into different food areas, one street crammed with hanging ducks and geese, another offering bright green vegetables or bunches of freshly picked herbs. The Chinese are extremely knowledgeable shoppers, taking their time to compare the quality of food on offer, planning their cooking around seasonal specialities, from clusters of lychees to live hairy crabs. Freshness is the Chinese mantra when it comes to food, and seafood is bought from a bed of shaved ice or plucked live from fish tanks, while chickens are beheaded and plucked to order. The wet market, which also sells a wide variety of dried foods, takes its name not from the fresh nature of the goods on offer, but from the way the stallholders hose down their fruit, vegetables and fish, clearing away debris from the market and making their produce sparkle.

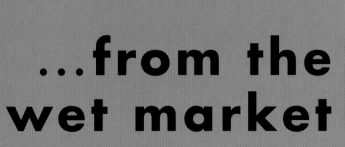

...from the wet market

mussels with
black bean sauce

1 kg (2 lb 4 oz) mussels
1 tablespoon oil
1 garlic clove, finely chopped
½ teaspoon finely chopped ginger
2 spring onions (scallions), finely chopped
1 red chilli, chopped
1 tablespoon light soy sauce
1 tablespoon Shaoxing rice wine
1 tablespoon salted, fermented black
   beans, rinsed and mashed
2 tablespoons chicken and meat stock
   or recipe page 249
few drops of roasted sesame oil

Serves 4

Scrub the mussels, remove any beards, and throw away any that do not close when tapped on the work surface.

Place the mussels in a large dish in a steamer. Steam over simmering water in a covered wok for 4 minutes, discarding any that do not open after this time.

Meanwhile, heat the oil in a small saucepan. Add the garlic, ginger, spring onions and chilli and cook, stirring, for 30 seconds. Add the remaining ingredients, and blend well. Bring to the boil, then reduce the heat and simmer for 1 minute.

To serve, remove and discard the top shell of each mussel, pour 2 teaspoons of the sauce into each mussel and serve on the shell.

700 g (1 lb 9 oz) prawns (shrimp)
2 tablespoons Shaoxing rice wine
2 slices ginger, smashed with the
   flat side of a cleaver
3 teaspoons roasted sesame oil
1½ tablespoons cornflour (cornstarch)
120 ml (½ cup) oil
2 spring onions (scallions), white part
   only, finely chopped
1 tablespoon finely chopped ginger

2 garlic cloves, finely chopped
1 red capsicum (pepper), diced
1 green capsicum (pepper), diced
2½ tablespoons tomato sauce (ketchup)
2 tablespoons clear rice vinegar
2 tablespoons sugar
1 teaspoon light soy sauce
½ teaspoon salt

Serves 6

Peel the prawns, score each one along the length of the back so the prawns will 'butterfly' when cooked, and devein them. Place the prawns in a bowl and add the rice wine, ginger, 2 teaspoons of the sesame oil and 1 tablespoon of the cornflour. Pinch the ginger slices in the marinade repeatedly for several minutes to impart the flavour into the marinade. Toss lightly, then leave to marinate for 20 minutes. Discard the ginger slices and drain the prawns.

Heat a wok over high heat, add 2 tablespoons of the oil and heat until very hot. Add half the prawns and toss lightly over high heat for about 1½ minutes, or until the prawns turn pink and curl up. Remove with a wire sieve or slotted spoon and drain. Repeat with another 2 tablespoons of the oil and the remaining prawns. Pour off the oil and wipe out the wok.

Reheat the wok over high heat, add the remaining oil and heat until very hot. Add the spring onions, ginger and garlic and stir-fry for 15 seconds, or until fragrant. Add the red and green capsicum and stir-fry for 1 minute. Combine the tomato sauce, rice vinegar, sugar, soy sauce, salt and the remaining sesame oil and cornflour with 125 ml (½ cup) water, add to the sauce and simmer until thickened. Add the prawns and toss lightly to coat.

sweet-and-sour prawns

clams in yellow
bean sauce

**1.5 kg (3 lb 5 oz) hard-shelled clams
(vongole)**
1 tablespoon oil
2 garlic cloves, crushed
1 tablespoon grated ginger
2 tablespoons yellow bean sauce
**125 ml (½ cup) chicken stock
or recipe page 249**
1 spring onion (scallion), sliced

Serves 4

Wash the clams in several changes of cold water, leaving them for a few minutes each time to remove any grit. Scrub the clams well, discarding any that remain open. Drain well.

Heat a wok over high heat, add the oil and heat until very hot. Stir-fry the garlic and ginger for 30 seconds, then add the bean sauce and clams and toss together. Add the stock and stir for 3 minutes until the clams have opened, discarding any that do not open after this time. Season with salt and white pepper.

Transfer the clams to a plate and sprinkle with spring onion.

16 king prawns
oil, for deep-frying
1 tablespoon oil, extra
1 garlic clove, finely chopped
½ teaspoon finely chopped ginger
1 tablespoon light soy sauce
1 tablespoon Shaoxing rice wine
1 tablespoon chilli bean paste (toban jiang)
1 teaspoon sugar
3–4 tablespoons chicken and meat stock
  or recipe page 249
1 teaspoon clear rice vinegar
1 spring onion (scallion), finely chopped
2 red chillies, finely chopped
¼ teaspoon roasted sesame oil
2 teaspoons cornflour (cornstarch)
coriander (cilantro) leaves

Serves 4

Pull off the legs from the prawns, but leave the body shells on. Using a pair of scissors, cut each prawn along the back to devein it.

Fill a wok to one-quarter full of oil. Heat the oil to 190°C (375°F/Gas 5), or until a piece of bread fries golden brown in 10 seconds when dropped in the oil. Cook the prawns in batches for 2 minutes, or until they turn bright orange. Remove and drain. It is important to keep the oil hot for each batch or the shells will not turn crisp. Pour off the oil and wipe out the wok.

Reheat the wok over high heat, add the extra oil and heat until very hot. Cook the garlic and ginger for a few seconds to flavour the oil. Add the soy sauce, rice wine, chilli bean paste, sugar and stock. Stir to combine, then bring to the boil. Add the prawns and cook for 1 minute, then add the rice vinegar, spring onion, chilli and sesame oil, stirring constantly. Combine the cornflour with enough water to make a paste, add to the sauce and simmer until thickened. Serve sprinkled with the coriander leaves, and provide finger bowls.

sichuan-style braised prawns

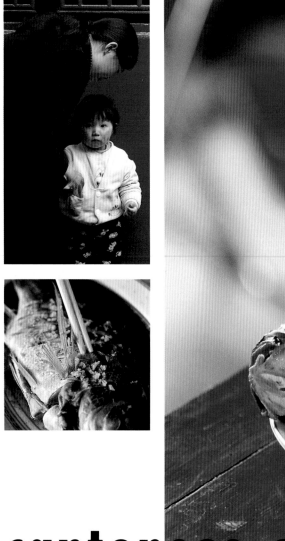

cantonese-style
steamed fish

750 g–1 kg (1 lb 10 oz–2 lb 4 oz) whole
   fish, such as carp, bream, grouper or
   sea bass
2 tablespoons Shaoxing rice wine
1½ tablespoons light soy sauce
1 tablespoon finely chopped ginger
1 teaspoon roasted sesame oil
2 tablespoons oil
2 spring onions (scallions), finely shredded
3 tablespoons finely shredded ginger
¼ teaspoon freshly ground black pepper

Serves 4

If you do manage to buy a swimming (live) fish, then ask the fishmonger to gut it through the gills. This is harder than gutting through the stomach, but leaves the fish looking whole. If you are gutting the fish yourself, make a cut from the throat to the tail and pull out the guts through the stomach. Remove any scales with a fish scaler or the back of a knife. Check that the gills have been cut out, then rinse the fish under cold running water and drain thoroughly in a colander.

Place the fish in a large bowl. Add the rice wine, soy sauce, chopped ginger and sesame oil, and toss lightly to coat. Cover with plastic wrap and leave to marinate in the fridge for 10 minutes.

Arrange the fish on a heatproof plate, with the marinade, and place in a steamer. Steam over simmering water in a covered wok for 5–8 minutes, or until the fish flakes when the skin is pressed firmly or the dorsal fin pulls out easily. Remove the fish from the steamer and place on a heatproof platter.

Heat a wok over high heat, add the oil and heat until smoking. Sprinkle the fish with the spring onion, shredded ginger and pepper, and slowly pour the hot oil over the fish. This will cause the skin to crisp, and cook the garnish.

wok... A Chinese meal can involve complex preparation: five or six dishes, each one a contrast in taste and texture, and all needing to be brought to the table together. Despite this, the Chinese kitchen is surprisingly simple, with meals cooked over just two gas burners using sometimes only one utensil, the wok. This one utensil is much more than a large Chinese frying pan. The wok shapes the nature of Chinese food as much as the ingredients that go into it, and Chinese cooks use it not just for stir-frying, but for deep-frying, blanching and steaming.

The heavy, deep cast-iron or carbonized steel woks found in China are heated to fierce temperatures never seen in Western kitchens; just a little oil is added to sear the food almost on contact. This short cooking time keeps meat and fish tender and vegetables crisp and vibrant, retaining their natural flavour and vitamins. Chinese chefs don't, in fact, stir-fry at all, but continually toss and flip ingredients high so they cook evenly, landing back into the curved base where the heat is at its most intense.

The very efficiency of the wok does, however, impose rules on its user. Preparation of food must be done in advance and can be time-consuming. Ingredients are cut small to prevent them from burning on the outside before they cook through, and should be cut to a uniform shape for even cooking. Careful timing is paramount, as throwing all the ingredients in at the same time will leave the dish both over and undercooked.

The wok itself is almost a living ingredient, which actually adds to a dish's taste. The steel is never washed with soap but seasoned with oil until it builds up a thin coating of flavour known as a patina. In the hands of a master chef, the wok can produce some sensational results, such as a dish that's served up with 'wok's breath' (indicating it's been cooked at exactly the right heat) still on it.

1 kg (2 lb 4 oz) large scallops
2 tablespoons salted, fermented black
   beans, rinsed and mashed
2 garlic cloves, crushed
3 teaspoons finely chopped ginger
2 teaspoons sugar
2 teaspoons light soy sauce
2 tablespoons oyster sauce
2 tablespoons oil
2 spring onions (scallions), cut into
   2 cm (¾ in) lengths

Serves 6

Slice the small, hard white muscle off the side of each scallop and pull off
any membrane. Rinse the scallops and drain. Pull off the roes if you prefer.

Place the black beans, garlic, ginger, sugar, soy and oyster sauces in a bowl
and mix together.

Heat a wok over high heat, add the oil and heat until very hot. Stir-fry the
scallops and roes for 2 minutes, or until the scallops are cooked through and
opaque. Just before the scallops are cooked, add the spring onions. Transfer
the mixture to a sieve to drain.

Reheat the wok over medium heat. Stir-fry the black bean mixture for
1–2 minutes, or until aromatic. Return the scallops and spring onions to
the wok and toss together to combine.

scallops with black bean sauce

crabmeat fu rong

250 g (9 oz) crabmeat, picked over
¹/₂ teaspoon salt
4 egg whites, beaten
1 tablespoon cornflour (cornstarch)
4 tablespoons milk
oil, for deep-frying
100 ml (¹/₂ cup) chicken and meat stock
   or recipe page 249
¹/₂ spring onion (scallion), finely chopped
¹/₂ teaspoon grated ginger
2 tablespoons peas
1 teaspoon Shaoxing rice wine
¹/₄ teaspoon roasted sesame oil
coriander (cilantro) leaves

Serves 4

Flake the crabmeat and mix with the salt, egg white, cornflour and milk.
Blend well.

Fill a wok to one-quarter full of oil and heat to 190°C (375°F/Gas 5),
or until a piece of bread fries golden brown in 10 seconds when dropped
in the oil. Pour the crabmeat mixture into the wok in batches. Do not stir,
otherwise it will scatter, but gently stir the oil from the bottom of the wok so
the crabmeat mixture ('fu rong') rises to the surface. Remove each batch as
soon as it is set, without letting it go too brown, and drain. Pour off the oil
and wipe out the wok.

Reheat the wok over high heat until very hot, add the stock, bring to the boil
and add the spring onion, ginger, peas and rice wine. Add the sesame oil.
Pour over the fu rong and sprinkle with coriander.

1.2 kg (2 lb 12 oz) chicken
2 spring onions (scallions), cut into
    5 cm (2 in) lengths
5 coriander (cilantro) sprigs
¾ teaspoon salt
4 slices ginger, smashed with the flat
    side of a cleaver
¼ teaspoon black peppercorns
finely chopped spring onion (scallion)

DIPPING SAUCE
2 spring onions (scallions), sliced
1 tablespoon finely grated ginger
1 teaspoon salt
3 tablespoons oil
3 tablespoons light soy sauce
1–2 red chillies, sliced

Serves 4

Rinse the chicken, drain, and remove any fat from the cavity opening and around the neck. Cut off and discard the parson's nose. Place the chicken in a large clay pot or casserole. Add the spring onion, coriander, salt, ginger, peppercorns and enough water to cover the chicken. Cover and bring to the boil, then reduce the heat and simmer very gently for 30 minutes. Turn off the heat and leave the chicken for 10 minutes. Remove the chicken from the pot and drain well. Skim off any scum from the liquid and strain the liquid.

To make the dipping sauce, combine the spring onions, ginger and salt in one small heatproof or metal bowl.

Heat a wok over high heat, add the oil and heat until smoking. Allow it to cool slightly, then pour over the spring onion mixture. The mixture will splatter. Stir well. Combine the soy sauce and chilli in another small bowl.

Using a cleaver, cut the chicken through the bones into bite-size pieces. Pour the stock into soup bowls, sprinkle with the finely chopped spring onions, and serve with the chicken along with bowls of rice and the dipping sauce.

hainan chicken

crispy skin duck

2.25 kg (5 lb) duck
8 spring onions (scallions), ends trimmed,
   smashed with the flat side of a cleaver
8 slices ginger, smashed with the flat side
   of a cleaver
3 tablespoons Shaoxing rice wine
2 tablespoons salt
2 teaspoons Sichuan peppercorns
1 star anise, smashed with the flat side
   of a cleaver

2 tablespoons light soy sauce
120 g (1 cup) cornflour (cornstarch)
oil, for deep-frying
hoisin sauce
Mandarin pancakes (page 248)

Serves 6

Rinse the duck, drain, and remove any fat from the cavity opening and from around the neck. Cut off and discard the parson's nose. Combine the spring onions, ginger, rice wine, salt, Sichuan peppercorns and star anise. Rub the marinade all over the inside and outside of the duck. Place, breast-side-down, in a bowl with the remaining marinade and leave in the fridge for at least 1 hour. Put the duck and the marinade, breast-side-up, on a heatproof plate in a steamer, or cut into halves or quarters and put in several steamers.

Steam over simmering water in a covered wok for 1½ hours, replenishing with boiling water during cooking. Remove the duck, discard the marinade, and let cool. Rub the soy sauce over the duck, then dredge in the cornflour, pressing lightly to make it adhere to the skin. Let the duck dry in the fridge for several hours until very dry.

Fill a wok to one-quarter full of oil. Heat the oil to 190°C (375°F/Gas 5), or until a piece of bread fries golden brown in 10 seconds when dropped in the oil. Lower the duck into the oil and fry, ladling the oil over the top, until the skin is crisp and golden.

Drain the duck and, using a cleaver, cut the duck through the bones into pieces. Serve plain or with hoisin sauce and pancakes or bread.

1.5 kg (3 lb 5 oz) chicken
1 tablespoon ground Sichuan peppercorns
2 tablespoons grated ginger
2 tablespoons sugar
3 tablespoons Shaoxing rice wine
300 ml (1¼ cups) dark soy sauce
200 ml (¾ cup) light soy sauce
600 ml (2½ cups) oil
450 ml (1¾ cups) chicken and meat stock
   or recipe page 249
2 teaspoons roasted sesame oil

Serves 4

Rinse the chicken, drain, and remove any fat from the cavity opening and around the neck. Cut off and discard the parson's nose. Rub the peppercorns and ginger all over the inside and outside of the chicken. Combine the sugar, rice wine and soy sauces, add the chicken and marinate in the fridge for at least 3 hours, turning occasionally.

Heat a wok over high heat, add the oil and heat until very hot. Drain the chicken, reserving the marinade, and fry for 8 minutes until browned. Put in a clay pot or casserole dish with the marinade and stock. Bring to the boil, then simmer, covered, for 35–40 minutes. Leave off the heat for 2–3 hours, transferring to the fridge once cool. Drain the chicken, brush with oil and refrigerate for 1 hour.

Using a cleaver, chop the chicken through the bones into bite-size pieces, pour over a couple of tablespoons of sauce and serve.

soy chicken

soy sauce

Soy sauce is the ingredient that adds that unmistakable flavour to most Chinese food. One of the seven traditional necessities of a Chinese household, soy sauce joins tea, salt, oil, vinegar, rice and firewood as an item that, still today, no Chinese person can ever imagine living without.

Chinese dishes are always brought to the table ready to eat, the kitchen taking full responsibility for cutting up ingredients small enough to be plucked with chopsticks and carefully seasoning each dish. Thus, only in the South, with its simply cooked, delicately seasoned food, is soy sauce ever left on the table as a condiment. Unlike salt, its nearest Western equivalent, soy sauce interacts with the flavours in food, and in the kitchen it is added with care, chefs aware that its unique taste can easily mask more subtle flavours.

Soy sauce is extracted from soya beans, which surprisingly are named after the sauce, rather than the other way around. The cooked soya beans are mashed with wheat flour, then moulds are added to ferment the mixture. This process is known as natural brewing. Once mature, the liquid is strained and the final taste balanced by the aptly named 'soy sauce master'.

Soy sauce comes in more than just one form. Light soy is drawn from the first pressing and is added to white meat, fish and vegetables, imparting a delicate, salty flavour without colouring the dish. Dark soy is aged for longer and its stronger, sweeter flavour complements red meats. It's used in braises and red-cooking (braising in a soy-sauce-based liquid). Many Chinese dishes contain both types of sauces, the chef expertly adjusting the balance according to the recipe.

stir-fried beef
with spring onions

500 g (1 lb 2 oz) rump or
  sirloin steak, trimmed
2 garlic cloves, finely chopped
2 tablespoons light soy sauce
1 tablespoon Shaoxing rice wine
2 teaspoons sugar
1 tablespoon cornflour (cornstarch)
3 tablespoons oil
5 spring onions (scallions), green part only,
  cut into thin strips

SAUCE
3 tablespoons light soy sauce
2 teaspoons sugar
½ teaspoon roasted sesame oil

Serves 6

Cut the beef across the grain into slices that are 2 mm (⅛ in) thick, then cut into bite-size pieces. Combine in a bowl with the garlic, soy sauce, rice wine, sugar and cornflour. Marinate in the fridge for at least 1 hour. Drain.

To make the sauce, combine all the ingredients.

Heat a wok over high heat, add the oil and heat until very hot. Cook the beef in two batches for 1½ minutes each batch, or until brown. Remove and drain. Pour the oil from the wok, leaving 1 tablespoon.

Reheat the reserved oil over high heat until very hot and stir-fry the spring onions for 1 minute. Add the beef and the sauce. Toss to coat the meat and spring onions with the sauce.

750 g (1 lb 10 oz) rump or
   sirloin steak, trimmed
1 tablespoon light soy sauce
2 teaspoons Shaoxing rice wine
½ teaspoon roasted sesame oil
1 teaspoon cornflour (cornstarch)
250 ml (1 cup) oil

BLACK BEAN SAUCE
1 tablespoon oil
30 g (1 oz) finely chopped
   spring onion (scallion)
1 tablespoon finely chopped garlic
1 tablespoon salted, fermented black
   beans, rinsed and coarsely chopped

1 tablespoon finely chopped ginger
1 green capsicum (pepper), shredded
1 red capsicum (pepper), shredded
1 orange or yellow capsicum
   (pepper), shredded
2 teaspoons light soy sauce
1 tablespoon Shaoxing rice wine
1 teaspoon sugar
40 ml (2 tablespoons) chicken stock
   or recipe page 249
½ teaspoon roasted sesame oil
2 teaspoons cornflour (cornstarch)

Serves 6

Cut the beef across the grain into slices that are 1 mm (1/12 in) thick. Cut each slice of beef into thin strips and place in a bowl. Add the soy sauce, rice wine, sesame oil, cornflour and 1 tablespoon water, toss lightly to combine, then marinate in the fridge for 30 minutes. Drain the beef.

Heat a wok over high heat, add the oil and heat until almost smoking. Add a third of the beef and cook, stirring constantly, for 1 minute, or until the pieces brown. Remove with a wire sieve or slotted spoon, then drain. Repeat with the remaining beef.

To make the black bean sauce, heat a wok over high heat, add the oil and heat until very hot. Stir-fry the spring onion, garlic, black beans and ginger for 10 seconds, or until fragrant. Add the capsicum and stir-fry for 1 minute, or until cooked.

Combine the soy sauce, rice wine, sugar, stock, sesame oil and cornflour, add to the sauce and simmer until thickened. Add the beef and toss lightly to coat with the sauce.

beef with capsicum and black bean sauce

spareribs with sweet-and-sour sauce

500 g (1 lb 2 oz) Chinese-style
  pork spareribs
¼ teaspoon salt
¼ teaspoon freshly ground black pepper
1 teaspoon sugar
1 tablespoon Chinese spirit (Mou Tai)
  or brandy
1 egg yolk, beaten
1 tablespoon cornflour (cornstarch)
oil, for deep-frying

SAUCE
1 tablespoon oil
1 small green capsicum (pepper), shredded
3 tablespoons sugar
2 tablespoons clear rice vinegar
1 tablespoon light soy sauce
1 tablespoon tomato purée
¼ teaspoon roasted sesame oil
50 ml (2½ tablespoons) chicken and meat
  stock or recipe page 249
2 teaspoons cornflour (cornstarch)

Serves 4

Ask the butcher to cut the slab of spareribs crosswise into thirds that measure 4–5 cm (1½–2 in) in length, or use a cleaver to do so yourself. Cut the ribs between the bones to separate them. Put the pieces in a bowl with the salt, pepper, sugar and Chinese spirit. Marinate in the fridge for at least 35 minutes, turning occasionally.

Blend the egg yolk with the cornflour and enough water to make a thin batter. Remove the spareribs from the marinade and coat them with the batter.

Fill a wok to one-quarter full of oil. Heat the oil to 180°C (350°F/Gas 4), or until a piece of bread fries golden brown in 15 seconds when dropped in the oil. Fry the spareribs in batches for 5 minutes until they are crisp and golden, stirring to separate them, then remove and drain. Reheat the oil and fry the spareribs again for 1 minute to darken their colour. Remove and drain well on crumpled paper towels. Keep warm in a low-temperature oven.

To make the sauce, heat a wok over high heat, add the oil and heat until very hot. Stir-fry the capsicum for a few seconds, then add the sugar, rice vinegar, soy sauce, tomato purée, sesame oil and stock, and bring to the boil. Combine the cornflour with enough water to make a paste, add to the sauce and simmer until thickened. Add the spareribs and toss to coat them with the sauce. Serve hot.

a little taste of...

Chinese vegetarian food is not always quite what it seems. The Chinese are not great meat-eaters and in everyday cooking, vegetables predominate, particularly the glorious varieties of Chinese greens, from bok choy to Chinese broccoli. However, despite appearances, this is not vegetarian food. The dishes are invariably cooked in a chicken stock, flavoured with fish and oyster sauces or fried in animal oil. There is a long history of vegetarianism in China, but it is quite different from that in the West. Chefs go to extraordinary lengths to create dishes that imitate meat, poultry and seafood, often extremely realistically. This is Buddhist food, whose strict diet excludes eggs, dairy, garlic and onions, but which has nonetheless created an extremely sophisticated cuisine. Protein comes in the form of gluten and tofu, which add texture while soaking up flavour, while rich stocks are made from the liquid of soaking mushrooms. The chef's techniques are regarded as paramount and vegetables are beautifully cut and the food exquisitely presented. The creativeness and wonderful flavours of Buddhist cuisine has made vegetarian food an integral part of Chinese cooking.

...vegetable dishes

tofu and
spinach soup

120 g (5 oz) soft tofu, drained
100 g (3 handfuls) baby spinach leaves
1 litre (4 cups) chicken and meat stock
** or recipe page 249**
1 tablespoon light soy sauce

Serves 4

Cut the tofu into small slices about 5 mm (¼ in) thick. Chop the spinach leaves roughly if they are large.

Bring the stock to a rolling boil in a large clay pot or saucepan, then add the tofu and soy sauce. Return to the boil, then reduce the heat and simmer gently for 2 minutes. Skim any scum from the surface. Add the spinach and cook for 1–2 minutes. Season with salt and white pepper. Serve hot.

12 dried Chinese mushrooms
300 g (1¼ cups) fresh or tinned bamboo
    shoots, rinsed and drained
3 tablespoons oil
2 tablespoons light soy sauce
2 teaspoons sugar
2 teaspoons cornflour (cornstarch)
½ teaspoon roasted sesame oil

Serves 4

Soak the dried mushrooms in boiling water for 30 minutes, then drain, reserving the liquid, and squeeze out any excess water. Remove and discard the stems and cut the caps in half (or quarters if large). Cut the bamboo shoots into small pieces, the same size as the mushrooms.

Heat a wok over high heat, add the oil and heat until very hot. Stir-fry the mushrooms and bamboo shoots for 1 minute. Add the soy sauce and sugar, stir a few times, then add 100 ml (½ cup) of the reserved liquid. Bring to the boil and braise for 2 minutes, stirring constantly.

Combine the cornflour with enough water to make a paste, add to the sauce and simmer until thickened. Sprinkle with the sesame oil, blend well and serve.

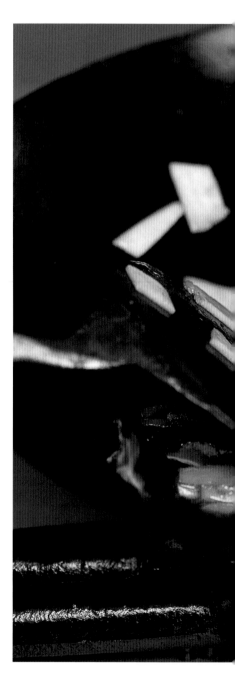

stir-fried twin winter

soft tofu with chilli

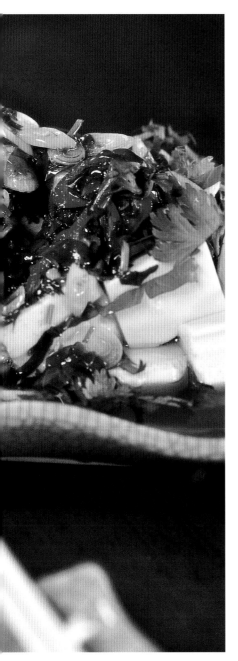

250 g (9 oz) soft tofu, drained
2 spring onions (scallions), thinly sliced
1 red chilli, thinly sliced
2 tablespoons chopped coriander (cilantro)
2 tablespoons soy sauce
80 ml (¹/₃ cup) oil
1 teaspoon roasted sesame oil

Serves 4

Cut the tofu into cubes and put on a heatproof plate.

Scatter the spring onions, chilli, coriander and soy sauce over the tofu. Put the oils in a small saucepan and heat until they are smoking, then immediately pour the oils over the tofu.

chillies

Compared to the rest of Asia, the cooking of China uses surprisingly few herbs and spices. In the South, the emphasis is on letting extremely fresh ingredients, prepared simply, speak for themselves, while in the East and North, there are stronger tastes. However, these come from the essential flavourings of all Chinese kitchens: soy sauce, rice wine and vinegars, bean pastes and sesame oil.

Only one region rivals, perhaps even surpasses, the rest of Asia for its spicy, hot dishes. The people of the western provinces of Sichuan and Hunan are China's chilli fiends, their cuisine so hot that their much-loved hotpot, the broth

laced with chilli oil, is almost inedible to outsiders. Chillies are not native to China; they were imported from the New World. But the Sichuanese enthusiastically embraced them, praising their medicinal and nutritional values and mixing them with the local tongue-numbing Sichuan pepper to create, despite the heat, a wonderfully complex cuisine. Sichuan dishes aim for that perfect blend of sweet, sour, salty, peppery and chilli hot, and when it works, as in dishes like hot-and-sour soup and *ma po tofu*, the result is a combination of searing heat with an incredible fragrance and contrast of textures.

1 kg (2 lb 4 oz) Chinese broccoli (gai lan)
1½ tablespoons oil
2 spring onions (scallions), finely chopped
1½ tablespoons grated ginger
3 garlic cloves, finely chopped
3 tablespoons oyster sauce
1½ tablespoons light soy sauce
1 tablespoon Shaoxing rice wine
1 teaspoon sugar
1 teaspoon roasted sesame oil
120 ml (½ cup) chicken stock
   or recipe page 249
2 teaspoons cornflour (cornstarch)

Serves 6

Wash the broccoli well. Discard any tough-looking stems and diagonally cut into 2 cm (¾ in) pieces through the stem and the leaf. Blanch the broccoli in a pan of boiling water for 2 minutes, or until the stems and leaves are just tender, then refresh in cold water and dry thoroughly.

Heat a wok over high heat, add the oil and heat until very hot. Stir-fry the spring onions, ginger and garlic for 10 seconds, or until fragrant. Add the broccoli and cook until the broccoli is heated through. Combine the remaining ingredients, add to the wok, stirring until the sauce has thickened, and toss to coat the broccoli.

chinese broccoli in oyster sauce

northern-style tofu

1 kg (2 lb 4 oz) firm tofu, drained
oil, for deep-frying
120 g (1 cup) cornflour (cornstarch)
2 eggs, lightly beaten
1 tablespoon finely chopped ginger
350 ml (1½ cups) chicken stock
    or recipe page 249
2 tablespoons Shaoxing rice wine
1 teaspoon salt, or to taste
½ teaspoon sugar
1½ teaspoons roasted sesame oil
2 spring onions (scallions), green part
    only, finely chopped

Serves 6

Holding a cleaver parallel to the cutting surface, slice each tofu cake in half horizontally. Cut each piece into 3 cm (1 in) squares.

Fill a wok to one-quarter full of oil. Heat the oil to 190°C (375°F/Gas 5), or until a piece of bread fries golden brown in 10 seconds when dropped in the oil. Coat each piece of tofu in the cornflour, then dip in the beaten egg to coat. Cook the tofu in batches for 3–4 minutes on each side, or until golden brown. Remove with a wire sieve or slotted spoon and drain in a colander. Pour the oil from the wok, leaving 1 teaspoon.

Reheat the reserved oil over high heat until very hot and stir-fry the ginger for 5 seconds, or until fragrant. Add the stock, rice wine, salt and sugar, and bring to the boil. Add the fried tofu and pierce the pieces with a fork so they will absorb the cooking liquid. Cook over medium heat for 20 minutes, or until all the liquid is absorbed. Drizzle the sesame oil over the tofu, toss carefully to coat, sprinkle with the spring onions and serve.

400 g (1 bunch) bok choy (pak choi)
2 tablespoons oil
2 garlic cloves, smashed with
the flat side of a cleaver
3 thin slices ginger, smashed with
the flat side of a cleaver
3 tablespoons chicken stock
or recipe page 249
1 teaspoon sugar
salt or light soy sauce, to taste
1 teaspoon roasted sesame oil

Serves 4

Cut the bok choy into 5–8 cm (2–3 in) lengths. Trim off any roots that may hold the pieces together, then wash well and dry thoroughly.

Heat a wok over high heat, add the oil and heat until very hot. Stir-fry the garlic and ginger for 30 seconds. Add the bok choy and stir-fry until it begins to wilt, then add the stock and sugar and season with the salt or soy sauce. Simmer, covered, for 2 minutes, or until the stems and leaves are tender but still green. Add the sesame oil and serve hot.

stir-fried bok choy

double-cooked yard-long beans

1 kg (2 lb 4 oz) yard-long (snake) beans
    or French beans, trimmed
150 g (6 oz) minced pork or beef
2 tablespoons light soy sauce
1½ tablespoons Shaoxing rice wine
½ teaspoon roasted sesame oil
oil, for deep-frying
5 tablespoons finely chopped
    preserved mustard cabbage
3 spring onions (scallions), finely chopped
1½ teaspoons sugar

Serves 6

Diagonally cut the beans into 5 cm (2 in) pieces. Lightly chop the minced meat with a cleaver until it goes slightly fluffy. Put the meat in a bowl, add 1 teaspoon of the soy sauce, 1 teaspoon of the rice wine and the sesame oil and stir vigorously to combine.

Fill a wok to one-quarter full of oil. Heat the oil to 180°C (350°F/Gas 4), or until a piece of bread fries golden brown in 15 seconds when dropped in the oil. Add a third of the beans, covering the wok with the lid as they are placed in the oil to prevent the oil from splashing. Cook for 3½–4 minutes, stirring constantly, until they are tender and golden brown at the edges. Remove with a wire sieve or slotted spoon and drain. Reheat the oil and repeat with the remaining beans. Pour the oil from the wok, leaving 1 tablespoon.

Reheat the reserved oil over high heat until very hot, add the minced meat and stir-fry until the colour changes, mashing and chopping to separate the pieces of meat. Push the meat to the side and add the preserved mustard cabbage and spring onions. Stir-fry over high heat for 15 seconds, or until fragrant. Add the beans with the remaining soy sauce and rice wine, sugar and 1 tablespoon water, and return the meat to the centre of the pan. Toss lightly to coat the beans with the sauce.

4 eggs
2 teaspoons roasted sesame oil
1 tablespoon oil
2 spring onions (scallions), finely chopped
2 large very ripe tomatoes,
   roughly chopped

Serves 4

Beat the eggs with the sesame oil and season with salt. Heat a wok or non-stick frying pan over high heat, add the oil and heat until very hot. Stir-fry the spring onions for 30 seconds, then add the tomato and stir-fry for 30 seconds. Add the egg and stir until the egg is set.

stir-fried eggs and tomatoes

rice... A bowl of rice is revered in China, where a grain, *fan,* is always the star of a meal and the *cai,* meat, seafood, vegetables or pickles, are seen as secondary. Fried rice, so loved in the West, is never eaten as part of a meal in Chinese homes, and brown rice is almost unknown. Instead, the whole point of rice is not as a dish in itself, but in the way its pure white simplicity can bring the many elements of a Chinese meal together.

Historically, rice has been China's backbone. Able to support more people than any other crop, it is also an excellent source of kilojoules when other foods are scarce. Many Chinese people have eaten rice every day of their lives, and its

continued importance can be counted in rice cookers, in an increasingly consumerist society perhaps the most desirable of all appliances.

There is no history of eating uncooked food in China and it is not uncommon to eat rice at every meal, especially in the South where rice is grown. A typical breakfast is *congee*, a rice porridge that is the ultimate in Chinese comfort food. It is usually served simply, with garnishes to add yourself, perhaps a little pickle or salted egg.

The Chinese worker never scrimps on lunch either, and more often than not this is a rice plate, consisting of fluffy, steamed rice topped with a little stir-fried seafood and vegetables, or perhaps slices of barbecued meat. These meals are piled into polystyrene containers and delivered to the worker's office or picked up at lunchtime from the original Chinese take-away.

For dinner, rice is served in individual bowls, the diners treating it almost as a plate and piling shreds of meat, fish and vegetables on top from the table's shared platters. Only at a banquet or formal dinner does rice take a back seat, the Chinese eating out to enjoy the chef's more exotic and expensive delicacies.

salted soya
bean pods

300 g (11 oz) fresh soya bean pods
1 tablespoon coarse sea salt
4 star anise

Serves 4 as a snack

Top and tail the bean pods, then place in a bowl with the salt and rub some of the fuzz off the skin. Rinse the pods. Place in a saucepan of salted water with the star anise and bring to the boil. Reduce the heat and simmer for 20 minutes, or until tender. Drain and leave to cool.

To eat, simply suck the beans out of the pods and throw the pods away. Serve as a snack.

25 g (1 oz) tiger lily buds (golden needles)
6–8 dried Chinese mushrooms
10 g (1 cup) dried black fungus
  (wood ears)
150 g (6 oz) ready-made braised
  gluten, drained
50 g (2 oz) tofu puffs (deep-fried
  cubes of tofu)
100 g (1 cup) bean sprouts
1 carrot
4 tablespoons oil

50 g (½ cup) snowpeas (mangetout),
  ends trimmed
1 teaspoon salt
½ teaspoon sugar
4 tablespoons vegetable stock
  or recipe page 249
2 tablespoons light soy sauce
½ teaspoon roasted sesame oil

Serves 4

Soak the lily buds in boiling water for 30 minutes. Rinse and drain the lily buds, and trim off any roots if they are hard. Soak the dried mushrooms in boiling water for 30 minutes, then drain and squeeze out any excess water. Remove and discard the stems and cut the caps in half (or quarters if large). Soak the dried black fungus in cold water for 20 minutes, then drain and squeeze out any excess water. Cut any large pieces of fungus in half.

Cut the gluten and tofu into small pieces. Wash the bean sprouts, discarding any husks and straggly end pieces, and dry thoroughly. Diagonally cut the carrot into thin slices.

Heat a wok over high heat, add the oil and heat until very hot. Stir-fry the carrot for 30 seconds, then add the snowpeas and bean sprouts. Stir-fry for 1 minute, then add the gluten, tofu, lily buds, mushrooms, fungus, salt, sugar, stock and soy sauce. Toss everything together, then cover and braise for 2 minutes at a gentle simmer.

Add the sesame oil, toss it through the mixture and serve hot or cold.

buddha's delight

sichuan
pickled cucumber

200 g (7 oz) cucumbers
½ teaspoon salt
30 g (1 oz) ginger, finely shredded
½ small red chilli, seeded and finely
    shredded
3 tablespoons roasted sesame oil
½ teaspoon Sichuan peppercorns
6 dried chillies, seeded and cut into
    5 mm (¼ in) lengths
1½ tablespoons clear rice vinegar
1½ tablespoons sugar

Serves 6 as a snack

Cut the cucumbers in half lengthways, remove the seeds, and cut into slices that are 6 cm (2¼ in) long and 2 cm (¾ in) thick. Place in a bowl, add the salt, toss lightly and leave for 30 minutes. Place the ginger in a bowl and soak in cold water for 20 minutes.

Pour off any water that has accumulated with the cucumber, rinse the cucumber lightly, then drain thoroughly and pat dry. Place the cucumber in a bowl with the drained ginger and chilli.

Heat a wok over high heat, add the sesame oil and heat until very hot. Add the peppercorns and stir-fry for 15 seconds until fragrant. Add the dried chilli and stir-fry for 15 seconds, or until dark. Pour into the bowl with the cucumber, toss lightly and leave to cool. Add the vinegar and sugar, toss to coat, then leave in the fridge for at least 6 hours or overnight. Serve cold or at room temperature.

350 g (12 oz) pea shoots
1 teaspoon oil
2 garlic cloves, finely chopped
1½ tablespoons Shaoxing rice wine
¼ teaspoon salt

Serves 6

Trim the tough stems and wilted leaves from the pea shoots. Wash well and dry thoroughly.

Heat a wok over high heat, add the oil and heat until very hot. Add the pea shoots and garlic and toss lightly for 20 seconds, then add the rice wine and salt, and stir-fry for 1 minute, or until the shoots are slightly wilted, but still bright green. Transfer to a platter, leaving behind most of the liquid. Serve hot, at room temperature, or cold.

flash-cooked pea shoots with garlic

a little taste of...

The traditional *dai pai dongs* are a Hong Kong legend. Pavement restaurants, they trade out of mobile metal carts, flocking to night markets and setting up in busy alleyways between shops and bars. Indeed, their presence at the city's night-time waterfront once saw the area nicknamed 'the poor man's nightclub', as they plied their trade beside hawkers, magicians and fortune-tellers. Local street food is sold in a similar way all over China, but the *dai pai dong* specializes in its own brand of tasty Cantonese snacks: beef noodles, stinky tofu, chicken bits and fish balls. Customers sit outside at a few wobbly tables and can enjoy a beer from the neighbouring store with their late-night bowl of congee or won tons. In recent years, the government has been clearing these vendors from the city's congested streets, but their spirit lives on in tiny booths that form food halls above the wet markets and in busy pedestrian areas. Every person in Hong Kong has their favourite *dai pai dong* snack, and vendors can become famous for their specialities. Some connoisseurs will hunt down the city's best noodles, chilli crabs, clams or other favourites.

...street food

steamed breads

1 quantity basic yeast dough (page 251)
3 tablespoons roasted sesame oil

Makes 12 flower rolls or
6 silver-thread loaves

Cut the dough in half and, on a lightly floured surface, roll out each half to form a 30 x 10 cm (12 x 4 in) rectangle. Brush the surface of the rectangles liberally with the sesame oil. Place one rectangle directly on top of the other, with both oiled surfaces facing up. Starting with one of the long edges, roll up the dough swiss-roll style. Pinch the two ends to seal in the sesame oil.

Lightly flatten the roll with the heel of your hand and cut the roll into 5 cm (2 in) pieces. Using a chopstick, press down on the centre of each roll, holding the chopstick parallel to the cut edges. (This will cause the ends to 'flower' when they are steamed.) Arrange the shaped rolls well apart in four steamers lined with greaseproof paper punched with holes. Cover and let rise for 15 minutes.

Cover and steam each steamer separately over simmering water in a wok for 15 minutes, or until the rolls are light and springy. Keep the rolls covered until you are about to eat them to make sure they stay soft.

The dough can also be shaped in other ways, one of the most popular being silver-thread bread. Divide the dough in half and roll each half into a sausage about 3 cm (1 in) diameter, then cut each sausage into six pieces. Roll six of the dough pieces into rectangles 20 x 10 cm (8 x 4 in) and set aside. Roll the remaining pieces into rectangles 20 x 10 cm (8 x 4 in), brush each with a little sesame oil and fold in half to a 10 cm (4 in) square. Brush with more sesame oil and fold in half again. Cut into thin strips crossways. Place one of the rectangles on the work surface and stretch the strips so they fit down the centre. Fold the ends and sides in, to completely enclose the strips. Repeat with the remaining dough until you have six loaves. Steam as for the flower rolls for 20–25 minutes.

200 g (1 cup) short-grain rice
2 dried Chinese mushrooms
80 g (¾ cup) snowpeas (mangetout),
   ends trimmed
2 Chinese sausages (lap cheong)
2 tablespoons oil
¼ red onion, finely diced

1 carrot, cut into 1 cm (½ in) dice
2–2.25 litres (8–9 cups) chicken stock
   or recipe page 249 or water
¼ teaspoon salt
3 teaspoons light soy sauce

Serves 6

Put the rice in a bowl and, using your fingers as a rake, rinse under cold running water to remove any dust. Drain the rice in a colander.

Soak the dried mushrooms in boiling water for 30 minutes, then drain and squeeze out any excess water. Remove and discard the stems and chop the caps into 5 mm (¼ in) dice. Cut the snowpeas into 1 cm (½ in) pieces.

Place the sausages on a plate in a steamer. Cover and steam over simmering water in a wok for 10 minutes, then cut them into 1 cm (½ in) pieces.

Heat a wok over medium heat, add the oil and heat until hot. Stir-fry the sausage until it is brown and the fat has melted out of it. Remove with a wire sieve or slotted spoon and drain. Pour the oil from the wok, leaving 1 tablespoon.

Reheat the reserved oil over high heat until very hot. Stir-fry the red onion until soft and transparent. Add the mushrooms and carrot and stir-fry for 1 minute, or until fragrant.

Put the mushroom mixture in a clay pot, casserole dish or saucepan and stir in 2 litres (8 cups) of stock or water, the salt, soy sauce and the rice. Bring to the boil, then reduce the heat and simmer very gently, stirring occasionally, for 1¾–2 hours, or until it has a porridge-like texture and the rice is breaking up. If it is too thick, add the remaining stock and return to the boil. Toss in the snowpeas and sausage, cover and stand for 5 minutes before serving.

rainbow congee

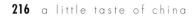

roast duck
noodle soup

450 g (1 lb) fresh or 350 g (12 oz)
   dried egg noodles
1 litre (4 cups) chicken stock or chicken
   and meat stock or recipe page 249
400 g (14 oz) roast duck, chopped
100 g (4 oz) bok choy (pak choi), shredded
2 tablespoons soy sauce
¼ teaspoon roasted sesame oil

Serves 4

Cook the noodles in a pan of salted boiling water for 2–3 minutes if fresh and 10 minutes if dried, then drain and place in four bowls. Bring the stock to a boil, then reduce the heat and keep at simmering point.

Top each bowl with the duck, bok choy, soy sauce and sesame oil, then pour on the stock.

24 chicken wings
3 lumps rock (lump) sugar
1 tablespoon dark soy sauce
1 tablespoon light soy sauce
1 tablespoon Shaoxing rice wine
oil, for deep-frying
2 teaspoons finely chopped ginger
1 spring onion (scallion), finely chopped
2 tablespoons hoisin sauce
150 ml (½ cup) chicken stock
    or recipe page 249

Serves 6

Discard the tip of each chicken wing. Cut each wing into two pieces through the joint. Put the wing pieces in a bowl.

Put the sugar, dark soy sauce, light soy sauce and rice wine in a small jug. Mix until combined, breaking the sugar down as much as you can. Pour the mixture over the chicken wings, then marinate in the fridge for at least 1 hour, or overnight.

Drain the chicken wings, reserving the marinade. Fill a wok to one-quarter full of oil. Heat the oil to 180°C (350°F/Gas 4), or until a piece of bread fries golden brown in 15 seconds when dropped in the oil. Cook the chicken wings in batches for 2–3 minutes, or until they are well browned. Drain on paper towels.

Carefully pour the oil from the wok, reserving 1 tablespoon. Reheat the wok over high heat, add the reserved oil and heat until very hot. Stir-fry the ginger and spring onion for 1 minute. Add the hoisin sauce, reserved marinade and chicken wings and cook for 1 minute, then add the stock and bring to the boil. Reduce the heat, cover the wok and cook gently for 8–10 minutes, or until the chicken wings are cooked through and tender.

Increase the heat and bring the sauce to the boil, uncovered. Cook until the sauce reduces to a sticky coating.

braised
chicken wings

spring
onion pancakes

250 g (2 cups) plain (all-purpose) flour
½ teaspoon salt
1 tablespoon oil
3 tablespoons roasted sesame oil
2 spring onions (scallions), green part
  only, finely chopped
oil, for frying

Makes 24

Place the flour and salt in a mixing bowl and stir to combine. Add the oil and 220 ml (1 cup) boiling water and, using a wooden spoon, mix to a rough dough. Turn the dough out onto a lightly floured surface and knead for 5 minutes, or until smooth and elastic. If the dough is very sticky, knead in a little more flour. Cover the dough with a cloth and let it rest for 20 minutes.

On a lightly floured surface, use your hands to roll the dough into a long roll. Divide the dough into 24 pieces. Working with one portion of dough at a time, place the dough, cut-edge-down, on the work surface. Using a small rolling pin, roll it out to a 10 cm (4 in) circle. Brush the surface generously with the sesame oil and sprinkle with some spring onion. Starting with the edge closest to you, roll up the dough and pinch the ends to seal in the spring onion and sesame oil. Lightly flatten the roll, then roll it up again from one end like a snail, pinching the end to seal it. Repeat with the remaining dough, sesame oil and spring onion. Let the rolls rest for 20 minutes.

Place each roll flat on the work surface and press down with the palm of your hand. Roll out to a 10 cm (4 in) circle and place on a lightly floured tray. Stack the pancakes between lightly floured sheets of baking paper and leave to rest for 20 minutes.

Heat a frying pan over medium heat, brush the surface with oil, and add two or three of the pancakes at a time. Cook for 2–3 minutes on each side, turning once, until the pancakes are light golden brown and crisp. Remove and drain on paper towels. Serve immediately.

You can reheat the pancakes, wrapped in foil, in a 180°C (350°F/Gas 4) oven for 15 minutes.

MARINADE
1 tablespoon rock (lump) sugar
1 tablespoon yellow bean sauce
1 tablespoon hoisin sauce
1 tablespoon oyster sauce
1 tablespoon red fermented tofu
1 tablespoon Chinese spirit (Mou Tai)
   or brandy
½ teaspoon roasted sesame oil

750 g (1 lb 10 oz) centre-cut
   pork loin, trimmed
2 tablespoons maltose or honey,
   dissolved with a little water

Serves 4

To make the marinade, combine the ingredients. Cut the pork into 4 x 20 cm (8 in) strips, add to the marinade and leave in the fridge for at least 6 hours.

Preheat the oven to 220°C (425°F/Gas 7). Put a baking dish filled with 600 ml (2½ cups) boiling water in the bottom of the oven. Drain the pork, reserving the marinade. Put an S-shaped meat hook through one end of each strip and hang from the top rack.

Cook for 10–15 minutes, then baste with the marinade. Reduce the heat to 180°C (350°F/Gas 4) and cook for 8–10 minutes. Cool for 2–3 minutes, then brush with the maltose and lightly brown under a grill for 4–5 minutes, turning to give a charred look around the edges.

Cut the meat into slices. Pour 200 ml (¾ cup) liquid from the dish into the marinade. Bring to the boil and cook for 2 minutes. Strain and pour over the pork.

char siu

char siu

The Chinese love to eat out, not just because they enjoy letting someone else do the cooking, but to sample the specialities that are impossible to prepare in domestic kitchens. Few homes own the oven needed to roast meats, and restaurants all over China, and especially in the South, cater for people craving a little roast duck, goose or *char siu*, honey-roasted pork.

These restaurants aren't difficult to spot, their windows full of whole birds and pieces of red pork hanging up to dry, an enticing aroma of marinating spices emanating from the large, cylindrical roasting ovens. Inside, the restaurants can be very basic, often just a few wooden tables and fold-up chairs.

Despite the large selection of meat hanging up, most customers order sparingly, perhaps combining some slices of roast duck with a noodle soup, or topping a bowl of steamed rice with fresh bok choy and chunks of tender *char siu*, its charred, caramelized crust giving the meat its common name, barbecue pork. Most of the restaurants also deal in take-away, customers often queueing outside at a counter for a little plastic tub of pork or duck to take home for dinner.

tea eggs

10 very fresh eggs or 20 quail eggs

TEA COOKING MIXTURE
3 tablespoons light soy sauce
3 tablespoons Shaoxing rice wine
1 star anise
1 tablespoon sugar
1 cinnamon stick
3 slices ginger, smashed
    with the flat side of a cleaver
3 tablespoons black Chinese tea leaves

Makes 10 eggs or 20 quail eggs

Place the eggs in a saucepan with enough cold water to cover. Bring the water to the boil, then reduce the heat to low and let the eggs simmer for 10 minutes, or until they are hard-boiled. Refresh the eggs in cold water. Drain the eggs and lightly tap and roll the shells on a hard surface to crack them. Do not remove the shells.

Put the tea cooking mixture ingredients in a heavy-based clay pot, casserole dish or saucepan with 1 litre (4 cups) water and heat until boiling. Reduce the heat to low and simmer for 20 minutes. Add the cooked eggs and simmer for 45 minutes. Turn off the heat and let the eggs sit in the tea mixture until cool enough to handle. Remove the shells and serve the eggs warm or cold, cut into wedges, with some of the cooking mixture on top.

PORK FILLING
350 g (12 oz) barbecue pork
   (char siu), chopped
3 spring onions (scallions), finely chopped
2 tablespoons chopped coriander (cilantro)

OR

PRAWN FILLING
250 g (9 oz) small prawns (shrimp)
1 tablespoon oil
3 spring onions (scallions), finely chopped
2 tablespoons chopped coriander (cilantro)

OR

VEGETABLE FILLING
300 g (11 oz) Chinese broccoli (gai lan)
1 teaspoon light soy sauce
1 teaspoon roasted sesame oil
2 spring onions (scallions), chopped

4 fresh rice noodle rolls
oyster sauce

Makes 4

To make the pork filling, combine the pork with the spring onions and coriander.

To make the prawn filling, peel and devein the prawns. Heat a wok over high heat, add the oil and heat until very hot. Stir-fry the prawns for 1 minute, or until they are pink and cooked through. Season with salt and white pepper. Add the spring onions and coriander and mix well.

To make the vegetable filling, wash the broccoli well. Discard any tough-looking stems and chop the rest of the stems. Put on a plate in the steamer, cover and steam over simmering water in a wok for 3 minutes, or until the stems and leaves are just tender. Combine the Chinese broccoli with the soy sauce, sesame oil and spring onions.

Carefully unroll the rice noodle rolls (don't worry if they crack or tear a little at the sides). Trim each one into a rectangle about 15 x 18 cm (6 x 7 in) (you may be able to get two out of one roll if they are very large). Divide the filling among the rolls, then re-roll the noodles. Put the rolls on a plate in a large steamer, cover and steam over simmering water in a wok for 5 minutes. Serve the rolls cut into pieces and drizzled with the oyster sauce.

steamed rice noodle rolls

char siu
noodle soup

4 dried Chinese mushrooms
200 g (7 oz) barbecue pork (char siu)
100 g (⅓ cup) fresh or tinned bamboo
   shoots, rinsed and drained
100 g (4 oz) green vegetable,
   such as spinach, bok choy (pak choi)
   or Chinese cabbage
2 spring onions (scallions)
450 g (1 lb) fresh or 350 g (12 oz)
   dried egg noodles
1 litre (4 cups) chicken and meat stock
   or recipe page 249
2–3 tablespoons oil
1 teaspoon salt
½ teaspoon sugar
1 tablespoon light soy sauce
1 teaspoon Shaoxing rice wine
¼ teaspoon roasted sesame oil

Serves 4

Soak the dried mushrooms in boiling water for 30 minutes, then drain and squeeze out any excess water. Remove and discard the stems and shred the caps. Thinly shred the pork, bamboo shoots, green vegetable and spring onions.

Cook the noodles in a pan of salted boiling water for 2–3 minutes if fresh and 10 minutes if dried, then drain and place in four bowls. Bring the stock to the boil, then reduce the heat to simmering.

Heat a wok over high heat, add the oil and heat until very hot. Stir-fry the pork and half the spring onions for 1 minute, then add the mushrooms, bamboo shoots and green vegetable, and stir-fry for 1 minute. Add the salt, sugar, soy sauce, rice wine and sesame oil and blend well.

Pour the stock over the noodles and top with the meat mixture and the remaining spring onion.

750 g (1 lb 10 oz) belly pork, rind on
1 teaspoon salt
1 teaspoon five-spice powder

DIPPING SAUCE
2 tablespoons light soy sauce
1 tablespoon dark soy sauce
1 tablespoon chilli sauce or
  recipe page 250 (optional)

Serves 6

Scrape the pork rind to make sure it is free of any bristles. Dry the rind, then rub with the salt and five-spice powder. Leave uncovered in the fridge for at least 2 hours.

To make the dipping sauce, combine all the ingredients.

Preheat the oven to 240°C (475°F/Gas 9). Place the pork, skin-side-up, on a rack in a roasting tin. Roast for 20 minutes, reduce the heat to 200°C (400°F/Gas 6) and cook for 40–45 minutes until crispy. Cut into pieces and serve with the sauce.

spicy crispy pork

noodles with beef and chives

250 g (9 oz) rump or
   sirloin steak, trimmed
2 large garlic cloves, crushed
3 tablespoons oyster sauce
2 teaspoons sugar
1 tablespoon dark soy sauce
3 teaspoons cornflour (cornstarch)
¼ teaspoon roasted sesame oil
3 tablespoons oil
1 red capsicum (pepper), thinly sliced
150 g (1 bunch) Chinese garlic chives,
   cut into 5 cm (2 in) lengths
1 kg (2 lb 4 oz) fresh rice noodle rolls,
   cut into slices 1.5–2 cm (½–¾ in) thick
   and separated slightly
chilli sauce or recipe page 250

Serves 6

Cut the beef across the grain into thin bite-size strips. Combine with the garlic,
1 tablespoon of the oyster sauce, 1 teaspoon of the sugar, 2 teaspoons of
the soy sauce, the cornflour and sesame oil. Marinate in the fridge for at least
30 minutes, or overnight.

Heat a wok over high heat, add the oil and heat until very hot. Stir-fry the
capsicum for 1–2 minutes, or until it begins to soften. Add the beef and
toss until it changes colour. Add the garlic chives and noodles and toss for
1–2 minutes, or until they soften. Add the remaining oyster sauce, sugar and
soy sauce and toss well until combined.

Serve with chilli sauce on the side.

2 tablespoons dried shrimp
300 g (11 oz) rice vermicelli
100 g (4 oz) barbecue pork (char siu)
100 g (1 cup) bean sprouts
4 tablespoons oil
2 eggs, beaten
1 onion, thinly sliced
1 teaspoon salt
1 tablespoon Chinese curry powder
2 tablespoons light soy sauce
2 spring onions (scallions), shredded
2 red chillies, shredded

Serves 4

Soak the dried shrimp in boiling water for 1 hour, then drain. Soak the noodles in hot water for 10 minutes, then drain. Thinly slice the pork. Wash the bean sprouts and drain thoroughly.

Heat a wok over high heat, add 1 tablespoon of the oil and heat until very hot. Pour in the egg and make an omelette. Remove from the wok and cut into small pieces.

Reheat the wok over high heat, add the remaining oil and heat until very hot. Stir-fry the onion and bean sprouts with the pork and shrimp for 1 minute, then add the noodles, salt, curry powder and soy sauce. Blend well and stir for 1 minute. Add the omelette, spring onion and chilli and toss to combine.

singapore noodles

noodles

Noodles are China's snack food. Not grand enough for restaurants, this is basic home-style fare, slurped up in a broth, boiled or fried. Local specialities, from Cantonese won tons to Sichuan's 'ants climbing trees', a dish of minced pork and slippery mung bean vermicelli, are served at any time of day from street stalls, tea houses, roadside shacks and noodle cafés. In northern China, where wheat fields make noodles more of a staple than rice, you can even see fresh noodles being made by hand. A lasso of wheat dough is pulled by the chef until it splits into white threads. The cooked noodles are then sunk into a tasty stock and garnished with herbs, vegetables or small pieces of meat.

In the humid rice-growing South, pale rice sticks or whispery rice vermicelli might be on the menu, while dim sum restaurants serve up fat, sticky rice noodle rolls stuffed with pork or prawns. Noodles can also be made from mung beans or tofu but because they're not made from wheat or rice, they aren't considered 'true' noodles and are used instead as an ingredient. Egg noodles, another Cantonese speciality, are perhaps the stars of the noodle family. Thin, yellow bundles are thrown into stir-fries and chow mein the world over. In Japan, where they are known as ramen, they have an almost cult following, eaten in big bowls of soup or deep-fried to make the world's favourite Asian snack — instant noodles.

dan dan mian

1 tablespoon Sichuan peppercorns
200 g (7 oz) minced pork
50 g (2 oz) preserved turnip,
   rinsed and finely chopped
2 tablespoons light soy sauce
2 tablespoons oil
2 garlic cloves, crushed
2 tablespoons grated ginger
4 spring onions (scallions), finely chopped
2 tablespoons sesame paste or smooth
   peanut butter
2 tablespoons light soy sauce
2 teaspoons chilli oil
200 ml (¾ cup) chicken stock
   or recipe page 249
400 g (14 oz) thin wheat flour noodles

Serves 4

Dry-fry the Sichuan peppercorns in a wok or pan until brown and aromatic, then crush lightly. Combine the pork with the preserved turnip and soy sauce and leave to marinate for a few minutes. Heat a wok over high heat, add the oil and heat until very hot. Stir-fry the pork until crisp and browned. Remove and drain well.

Add the garlic, ginger and spring onions to the wok and stir-fry for 30 seconds, then add the sesame paste, soy sauce, chilli oil and stock and simmer for 2 minutes.

Cook the noodles in a pan of salted boiling water for 4–8 minutes, then drain well. Divide among four bowls, ladle the sauce over the noodles, then top with the crispy pork and Sichuan peppercorns.

250 g (9 oz) prawns (shrimp)
80 g (½ cup) peeled water chestnuts
250 g (9 oz) lean minced pork
3½ tablepoons light soy sauce
3½ tablespoons Shaoxing rice wine
1½ teaspoons salt
1½ teaspoons roasted sesame oil
½ teaspoon freshly ground black pepper
1 teaspoon finely chopped ginger
1½ tablespoons cornflour (cornstarch)

30 square or round won ton wrappers
1.5 litres (6 cups) chicken stock
    or recipe page 249
450 g (1 bunch) baby spinach, trimmed
    (optional)
2 spring onions (scallions), green part
    only, finely chopped

Serves 6

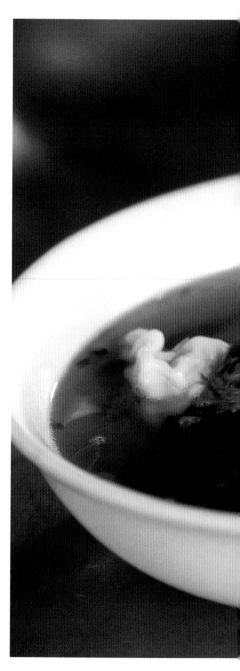

Peel and devein the prawns. Place in a tea towel and squeeze out as much moisture as possible. Mince the prawns to a coarse paste using a sharp knife or in a food processor.

Blanch the water chestnuts in boiling water for 1 minute, then refresh in cold water. Drain, pat dry and roughly chop them. Place the prawns, water chestnuts, pork, 2 teaspoons of the soy sauce, 2 teaspoons of the rice wine, ½ teaspoon of the salt, ½ teaspoon of the sesame oil, the black pepper, ginger and cornflour in a mixing bowl. Stir vigorously to combine.

Place a teaspoon of filling in the centre of one won ton wrapper. Brush the edge of the wrapper with a little water, fold in half, then bring the two folded corners together and press firmly. Place the won tons on a cornflour-dusted tray.

Bring a saucepan of water to the boil. Cook the won tons, covered, for 5–6 minutes, or until they have risen to the surface. Using a wire sieve or slotted spoon, remove the won tons and divide them among six bowls.

Place the stock in a saucepan with the remaining soy sauce, rice wine, salt and sesame oil, and bring to the boil. Add the spinach and cook until just wilted. Pour the hot stock over the won tons and sprinkle with the spring onions.

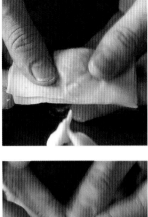

won ton soup

basics

MANDARIN PANCAKES

450 g (3½ cups) plain (all-purpose) flour
300 ml (1¼ cups) boiling water
1 teaspoon oil
roasted sesame oil

Makes 24–30

Sift the flour into a bowl, pour in the boiling water, stirring as you pour. Add the oil and knead into a firm dough. Cover with a damp tea towel and set aside for 30 minutes.

Turn the dough out onto a floured surface and knead for 8–10 minutes, or until smooth. Divide the dough into three equal portions, roll each portion into a long cylinder, then cut each cylinder into eight to 10 pieces. Roll each piece into a ball and press into a flat disc with the palm of your hand. Brush one disc with sesame oil and put another disc on top. Using a rolling pin, flatten each pair of discs into a 15 cm (6 in) pancake.

Heat an ungreased wok or frying pan over high heat, then reduce the heat to low and place the pairs of pancakes, one at a time, in the pan. Turn over when brown spots appear on the underside. When the second side is cooked, lift the pancakes out and carefully peel them apart. Fold each pancake in half with the cooked side facing inwards, and set aside under a damp cloth.

Just before serving, put the pancakes on a plate in a steamer. Cover and steam over simmering water in a wok for 10 minutes.

To store the pancakes, put them in the fridge for 2 days or in the freezer for several months. Reheat in a steamer for 4–5 minutes or in a microwave for 30–40 seconds.

CHICKEN AND MEAT STOCK

650 g (1 lb 7 oz) chicken carcasses, necks, pinions and feet
650 g (1 lb 7 oz) pork spareribs or veal bones
4 spring onions (scallions), ends trimmed,
   smashed with the flat side of a cleaver
12 slices ginger, smashed with the flat side of a cleaver
4 litres (16 cups) water
80 ml (⅓ cup) Shaoxing rice wine
2 teaspoons salt

Makes 3 litres (12 cups)

Remove excess fat from the chicken and meat, then chop into large pieces and place in a stockpot with the spring onions, ginger and water and bring to the boil. Reduce the heat and simmer for 3½–4 hours, skimming the surface to remove any impurities. Strain in a fine strainer, removing solids, and skim to remove any fat. If the stock is too weak, reduce it further. Store in the fridge for up to 3 days or freeze in small portions.

To make Chicken Stock, use 1.5 kg (3 lb 5 oz) chicken carcasses, necks, pinions and feet, 250 ml (1 cup) Shaoxing rice wine, 12 slices ginger, 6 spring onions (scallions) and 4 litres (16 cups) water. Follow the directions above, simmering for 3 hours.

VEGETABLE STOCK

500 g (1 lb 2 oz) fresh soya bean sprouts
10 dried Chinese mushrooms
6 spring onions (scallions), each tied into a knot
4 litres (16 cups) water
3 tablespoons Shaoxing rice wine
2 teaspoons salt

Makes 3 litres (12 cups)

Dry-fry the sprouts in a wok for 3 minutes. Place the sprouts, mushrooms, spring onions and water in a stockpot and bring to the boil. Reduce the heat and simmer for 1 hour. Strain in a fine strainer, removing the solids (keep the mushrooms for another use). Return to the pot with the rice wine and salt. Bring to the boil and simmer for 3–4 minutes. Store in the fridge for up to 3 days or freeze in small portions.

RED VINEGAR DIPPING SAUCE

125 ml (¹/₂ cup) red rice vinegar
3 tablespoons shredded
ginger

Makes 225 ml (about 1 cup)

Combine the rice vinegar, 2½ tablespoons water and the ginger in a small bowl, then divide among individual dipping bowls. This dipping sauce goes well with *jiaozi* (page 10).

SOY, VINEGAR AND CHILLI DIPPING SAUCE

125 ml (¹/₂ cup) light soy sauce
2 tablespoons Chinese black rice vinegar
2 red chillies, thinly sliced

Makes 200 ml (about ³/₄ cup)

Combine the soy sauce, vinegar and chilli in a small bowl, then divide among individual dipping bowls. This dipping sauce goes well with *jiaozi* (page 10) or a dim sum such as *har gau* (page 23) or tofu rolls (page 32).

CHILLI SAUCE

1 kg (2 lb 4 oz) red chillies, stalks removed
3 teaspoons salt
4 tablespoons sugar
160 ml (²/₃ cup) clear rice vinegar

Makes 400 ml (about 1²/₃ cups)

Put the chillies in a saucepan with 100 ml (¹/₂ cup) water, cover and bring to the boil. Cook until the chillies are tender, then add the salt, sugar and vinegar. Blend the chilli mixture to a paste in a blender or food processor, or push through a sieve. Store in the fridge for up to 1 month or freeze in small portions. You can use this chilli sauce as an ingredient or as a dipping sauce.

BASIC YEAST DOUGH

3 tablespoons sugar
250 ml (1 cup) warm water
1½ teaspoons dried yeast
**   or 10 g (¼ oz) fresh yeast**
400 g (3¼ cups) plain (all-purpose) flour
2 tablespoons oil
1½ teaspoons baking powder

Makes 1 quantity

Dissolve the sugar in the water, then add the yeast. Stir lightly, then set aside for 10 minutes, or until foamy.

Sift the flour into a bowl and add the yeast mixture and the oil. Using a wooden spoon, mix the ingredients to a rough dough. Turn the mixture out onto a lightly floured surface and knead for 8–10 minutes, or until the dough is smooth and elastic. If it is very sticky, knead in a little more flour—the dough should be soft. Lightly grease a bowl with the oil. Place the dough in the bowl and turn it so all sides of the dough are coated. Cover the bowl with a damp cloth and set aside to rise in a draught-free place for 3 hours.

Uncover the dough, punch it down, and turn it out onto a lightly floured surface. If you are not using the dough straightaway, cover it with plastic wrap and refrigerate.

When you are ready to use the dough, flatten it and make a well in the centre. Place the baking powder in the well and gather up the edges to enclose the baking powder. Pinch the edges to seal. Lightly knead the dough for several minutes to evenly incorporate the baking powder, which will activate immediately.

Use the prepared dough as directed.

glossary

abalone A single-shelled mollusc that is a delicacy in China. Sometimes it's available fresh from specialist fish shops, but more often used dried or tinned.

barbecue pork (*char siu*) A Cantonese speciality, these pork pieces are coated in maltose or honey and roasted until they have a red, lacquered appearance.

bean thread noodles Not true noodles, these are made from mung bean starch and are also labelled as cellophane or glass noodles. Soak before using.

black fungus Also known as wood or cloud ears, this fungus is dried in pieces and is available from Chinese shops.

bok choy (*pak choi*) This mild-flavoured cabbage has a fat white or pale green stem with dark green leaves.

Chinese broccoli (*gai lan*) This has dark-green stalks and leaves and tiny florets. It is widely available.

Chinese chives Garlic chives have a long, flat leaf and are green and very garlicky, or yellow with a milder taste.

Chinese mushrooms For a fresh version, use shiitake mushrooms. The Chinese usually use dried ones, which have a strong flavour and aroma. They need to be soaked before use. The soaking liquid can be used to flavour dishes.

Chinese pickles These are made from several types of vegetables, preserved in a brine or soy-based solution. They are available from Chinese shops.

Chinese sausage There are two kinds: *lap cheong* or *la chang*, which is made from pork and pork fat; and *yun cheung* or *xiang chang*, which is made from liver and pork. Chinese sausages must be cooked before eating.

Chinese spirits Distilled from grains, these are usually stonger than Western spirits. Brandy can be substituted.

Chinese-style pork spareribs These are the shorter, fatter ribs known as *pai gwat*. If they're unavailable, use any spareribs.

Chinese turnip This is actually a type of radish and is also known as Chinese white radish. It has a crisp, juicy flesh and mild radish flavour.

choy sum A green vegetable with a mild flavour often eaten with an oyster sauce.

dumpling wrappers Used for *jiaozi*, wheat wrappers, also called Shanghai wrappers or wheat dumpling skins, are white and can be round or square. Egg wrappers for *siu mai* are yellow and may also be round or square. Sometimes labelled as gow gee wrappers or egg dumpling skins. All are found in Chinese shops and good supermarkets.

gingko nuts These are the nuts of the maidenhair tree. The nuts are known for their medicinal properties. Shelled nuts can be bought in tins in Chinese shops and are easier to use.

gluten A wheat flour dough that has had the starch washed away so it is spongy and porous. It is used as a mock meat and is available from Chinese shops.

glutinous rice A short-grain rice that cooks to a sticky mass and so is used in dishes where the rice is required to hold together. Glutinous rice is labelled as such.

Guilin chilli sauce Made from salted, fermented yellow soya beans and chillies, it is used as an ingredient in cooking. Available from Chinese shops.

jujubes Also known as Chinese or red dates, jujubes are thought to build strength. They need to be soaked before use. They are also thought to be lucky because of their red colour.

longans From the same family as lychees, these are round with smooth, buff-coloured skins, translucent sweet flesh and large brown pips. Available fresh, tinned or dried.

lotus leaves The dried leaves of the lotus, they need to be soaked before use and are used for wrapping up food like sticky rice to hold it together while it is cooking. Available from Chinese shops.

lotus seeds These seeds from the lotus plant are considered medicinal. They are used in various dishes and are also roasted, salted or candied and eaten as a snack. Fresh and dried lotus seeds are available. Soak dried seeds before use.

maltose A sweet liquid of malted grains used to coat Peking Duck and barbecued meats. It is sold in Chinese shops, but honey can be used instead.

master sauce This is a basic stock of soy sauce, rice wine, rock sugar, spring onions, ginger and star anise. Additional ingredients vary according to individual chefs. Meat, poultry or fish is cooked in the stock, then the stock is reserved so it matures. The spices are replenished every three or so times the sauce is used. Master sauce spices can be bought as a mix, or a ready-made liquid version. Freeze between uses.

Mei Kuei Lu Chiew A fragrant spirit known as Rose Dew Liqueur. It is used in marinades. Brandy can be used instead.

preserved turnip This is Chinese turnip, sliced, shredded or grated, and usually preserved in brine. It needs to be rinsed before using so it is less salty.

rice vinegar Made from fermented rice, Chinese vinegars are milder than Western ones. Clear rice vinegar is mainly used for pickles and sweet-and-sour dishes. Red rice vinegar is a mild liquid used as a dipping sauce and served with shark's fin soup.

rock sugar Yellow rock sugar comes as uneven lumps of sugar. It is a pure sugar that gives a clear syrup and makes sauces it is added to shiny and clear. You can use sugar lumps (cubes) instead.

salted, fermented black beans These are very salty black soya beans that are fermented using the same moulds as those used for making soy sauce. Added to dishes as a flavouring, they must be rinsed before use.

Shaoxing rice wine Made from rice, millet, yeast and Shaoxing's local water, this is aged for at least three years. Dry sherry is the best substitute.

shark's fin Prized for its texture more than for its flavour, shark's fin is very expensive. Preparing a dried fin takes several days, so using the ready-made version is much easier.

Sichuan peppercorns Not a true pepper, but the berries of the prickly ash shrub. Unlike ordinary pepper, it has a pungent flavour and the aftertaste, rather than being simply hot, is numbing. The peppercorns should be crushed and dry-roasted to bring out their full flavour.

spring-roll wrappers Also called spring roll skins, these wrappers are readily available from supermarkets and can be frozen until needed.

steaming A method of cooking food in a moist heat to keep it tender and preserve its flavour. Bamboo steamers fit above a saucepan. You can stack them on top of each other, and reverse them halfway through cooking to ensure the cooking is even. Bamboo steamers are preferred in China as they absorb the steam, making the food a little drier.

tiger lily buds Sometimes called golden needles, these are bought dried and then soaked. They are used mainly in vegetarian dishes.

tofu puffs Deep-fried squares of bean curd, crispy on the outside and spongy in the middle. Puffs, sold in Chinese shops, can be frozen.

tofu skins These are made by scooping the layer of skin off the top of boiling soy milk. They come either as dried sheets, which need to be soaked in water, or already softened in vacuum packs.

wheat starch A powder-like flour made by removing the protein from wheat flour.

won ton wrappers Also called won ton skins, these are square and yellow and slightly larger than dumpling wrappers. They can be found in most supermarkets.

yard-long beans Also called snake or long beans, these are 40 cm long. The dark green ones have a firmer texture.

index

Published by Murdoch Books Pty Limited.
© Text, design, photography and illustrations Murdoch Books Pty Limited 2003. All rights reserved. First published 2003. Reprinted 2003, 2005.

Chief Executive: Juliet Rogers
Publisher: Kay Scarlett

Creative Director: Marylouise Brammer
Design Concept: Vivien Valk
Designer: Susanne Geppert
Food Editor: Lulu Grimes
Photographer: Jason Lowe
Stylist: Sarah de Nardi
Stylist's Assistants: Ross Dobson, Shaun Arantz, Olivia Lowndes
Recipes: Deh-Ta Hsiung, Nina Simonds
Editorial Director: Diana Hill
Editor: Carla Holt

National Library of Australia Cataloguing-in-Publication Data
A little taste of China. Includes index.
ISBN 1 74045 211 9.
1. Cookery, Chinese. 641.5951

PRINTED IN CHINA by Midas Printing (Asia) Ltd.

Murdoch Books Australia
Pier 8/9, 23 Hickson Road
Millers Point NSW 2000
Telephone: +61 (0) 2 8220 2000
Fax: +61 (0) 2 8220 2558

Murdoch Books UK Ltd
Erico House, 6th Floor North
93/99 Upper Richmond Road
Putney, London SW15 2TG
Telephone: + 44 (0) 20 8785 5995
Fax: + 44 (0) 20 8785 5985

IMPORTANT: Those who might be at risk from the effects of salmonella food poisoning (the elderly, pregnant women, young children and those suffering from immune deficiency diseases) should consult their GP with any concerns about eating raw eggs.